The Story of a Rare Parish

The Story
of a
Rare Parish

ST. CECILIA'S, BROOKLYN
1871–1930

BY
AGNES KING

Angelico Press

Cover design by
Michael Schrauzer

"It is the duty of those who have done or seen things worthy of remaining in the memory of man to record them."

      Baunard, translated by Stoddard

Dedicated to the memory of Right Reverend John Loughlin, D. D., first Bishop of Brooklyn, who laid the corner-stone of the first parish church and who laid the corner-stone of our present church; and to the memory of the Right Reverend Charles E. McDonnell, who officiated at the dedication and solemn consecration of St. Cecilia's; and to our present Right Reverend Bishop Thomas E. Molloy, D. D., whom may God long preserve to guide our Island Diocese in the path of divine truth and Christian charity.

EDWARD J. McGOLRICK,

Pastor.

June, 1931.

PREFATORY NOTE

Pastor's Message for the Angelico Press Edition (2021)

They say Brooklyn is "the borough of churches," and rightly so. Why? New York City and specifically Brooklyn was the first stop in the American experience for tens of millions of immigrants. These immigrants brought with them not only their hopes for a new and better life, but also their religion to sustain them and give meaning to their sufferings, sacrifices, and hopes for a better future for their children. Many sociologists note that immigrants also discovered or rediscovered the relevance of their own faith. In America, your Catholicism was not something you could take for granted as you could in the "old country." For the Catholic faith to take root in America one had to *practice* it, advocate for it, and actively contribute to its sustenance and survival. These immigrants from Ireland did so by putting their nickels and dimes together to build the magnificent structure we are privileged today to call our church.

St. Cecilia's Church was a community that touched every part of the life of its members under the visionary leadership of Msgr. Edward McGolrick (1857–1938). He was the Pastor of St. Cecilia's Church for 50 years from 1888 until the day he died while on a vacation in the country of his birth, Ireland, in 1938. Msgr. McGolrick built an impressive network of social support that touched practically every aspect of an immigrant's life: a maternity hospital, a day care center (the first of its kind in the country!), the largest Catholic parochial school building in America, a sports facility for her youth, housing for religious sisters and brothers, and charitable support for indigent burials. And of course, last but not least—in a borough filled with beautiful historic architecture—a church that is considered one of the most beautiful in all Brooklyn. It is a cathedral for the common man.

What follows in these pages is a testament to the love and faith of a people who put God, country, and service to the Catholic Church first in their lives. They faced and overcame innumerable obstacles in order for us to have the privilege of worshipping in the church that has survived to this day. This book is an inspiration for us all to continue tirelessly to serve in the vineyard of the Lord.

God Bless you all

God Bless, protect and preserve St. Cecilia's Church

FR. THOMAS VASSALOTTI
Pastor, Divine Mercy Parish
St. Cecilia/St. Francis of Paola/St. Nicholas

FOREWORD

The following pages present in attractive and impressive narrative the history of St. Cecilia's parish.

This historical sketch is very obviously the record of innumerable blessings bounteously bestowed by an infinitely good God; of unstinting and unselfish services rendered by zealous priests; of faithful devotion of religious men and women and of the sterling faith, extraordinary generosity and sacrifices of a truly loyal Catholic people.

These divine and human factors were indispensably required to realize and explain the exceptionally fruitful spiritual ministry and the most successful educational and charitable mission which this chronicle so justly and proudly assigns to what it chooses to describe, and, not without reason, as "a rare parish."

It is very interesting and indeed instructive to note that Monsignor McGolrick, who has administered St. Cecilia's so wisely and so well, was quick to understand that he should protect and promote not only the religious interests of his people but also their social, economic and physical welfare, since these latter phases of their life and experience might have a very harmful reaction upon their spiritual and moral progress.

And therefore with this prudent thought, wholesome purpose and truly priestly spirit he not only erected a magnificent church edifice and a splendid parish school but he also established a Social Settlement; Day Nursery; a Maternity Hospital and a well equipped recreational Center.

The distinguished pastor of St. Cecilia's has been favored with the rare blessing of having accomplished much for God and human souls and of being permitted now to enjoy the gratifying evidence of his notable achievements and the beneficent influence of his priestly ministry.

We sincerely hope and earnestly pray that God will continue thus to bless him so that with the aid of zealous assistants, devoted religious and a faithful people, he may promote for many years to come the great works of religion, education and of charitable relief and mercy.

† THOMAS E. MOLLOY,

Bishop of Brooklyn, N. Y.

The Story
of a
Rare Parish

ST. CECILIA'S PARISH.

Catholic parishes are established at the request of a number of Catholic families who claim that the nearest church is too distant for them to attend and who state that they can and will support a distinct church of their own. This petition goes before the Bishop and his Advisory Board and if favorable action is taken thereon then the Bishop sanctions the project and appoints a resident Pastor or places the new parish under the care of a neighboring Pastor. Thus St. Cecelia's was first placed under the care of Rev. John McDonald, Pastor of the Church of the Immaculate Conception, located at the corner of Leonard and Maujer Streets, and popularly known as St. Mary's.

A house was purchased in Herbert Street, midway between North Henry and Monitor Streets. A shed on the premises was annexed to this modest dwelling and the combined buildings served as St. Cecilia's earliest Church. Here the Holy Sacrifice was first offered on the beautiful Feast of the Immaculate Conception, December 8, 1870.

In the month of November 1871, the Right Rev. Bishop Loughlin, first Bishop of Brooklyn, laid the corner-stone of a frame Church building. The seating capacity of this house of God was four hundred.

For four years from the inception of the Parish, St. Cecilia's continued to be served from St. Mary's, a priest coming from there to offer two Masses on Sundays and Holy Days, one at eight and the other at ten-thirty o'clock, and to conduct catechism classes for the children in the hour following the first Mass.

Only recently in the now imposing St. Cecilia's occurred the funeral of one Mrs. Longein who, as Mary Rolph, came

from St. Mary's parish in the long ago to raise her girlish voice
in unison with her classmates in hymnal praise to God during
Mass in the humble little church.

There are no recorded facts of parish events from the lay-
ing of the corner-stone in 1871 until the occasion of the blessing of the church bell, donated by Mr. Thomas Riley, a retired
cotton merchant of the parish, on Sunday afternoon, March 31,
1873 the solemn blessing took place.

The local daily paper of that date devoted much space to
a complete and beautiful description of the ceremony, including an elaborate account of the antiquity of the custom. The
lengthy article is enlightening and breathes such reverential
spirit throughout, it is well worth inserting in this record of
St. Cecilia's Parish.

INTERESTING CHURCH CEREMONY.

Blessing of a Bell by Bishop Loughlin.—Antiquity of Custom.
Its Real Meaning.—The Use and Inspiration of Bells.
What the Poets Say.—Address by the Bishop.
The Ceremony. — The Name and
the Sponsors, etc.

———————

The Catholic Church of Saint Cecilia, corner of Herbert
and North Henry streets, was yesterday the scene of a specially
interesting ceremony, in which the Right Reverend Bishop
Loughlin of this diocese took the leading part. The occasion
was the solemn benediction of a bell, which has recently been
donated to the church by a worthy citizen of this district. And
here it may be mentioned, that the use of bells in Christian
churches, and their formal consecration to the divine service,

are matters of great antiquity. We have it on record that they were employed to call the faithful to prayer by St. Paulinus, Bishop of Campania, about the year 395; and

The Chronicles of Ancient Briton

mention that they were used by the Bishop of Llandaff, in Wales, in the middle of the sixth century. In point of fact, that which is distinctly called "Christian" architecture, embracing towers or steeples in all temples of worship, is indebted for this very feature to the necessity of having a suitable place wherein the church bell could be hung. The principal purposes for which the church bells are required, are thus quaintly expressed by an old English writer:

> To call the fold to Church in time,
>   We chime:
> When joy and mirth are on the wing,
>   We ring:
> When we lament the parted soul,
>   We toll.

Of the devotional or solemn feelings which the voice of the Church bell is calculated to inspire, the literature and poetry of all Christian countries are full of illustrations. The German poet, Schiller, has given to the Fatherland a beautiful

"Song of the Bells"

which is a good example, while Tennyson's "New Year" is not without some merit of the same sort. Among the American poets it may be noted, that the erratic genius of Poe has failed to suggest even a shadow of religious thought in his otherwise beautiful poem of the "The Bells"; while the more cultivated and reverential Longfellow, has discerned in their music the very message of the "Prince of Peace":

> I heard the bells on Christmas Day,
> Their old familiar carols play,
>> And wild and sweet,
>> The words repeat,
> Of "Peace on Earth, good will to men!"
> And thought how as the day had come,
> The belfries of all Christendom,
>> Had rolled along
>> The unbroken song,
> Of "Peace on earth, good will to men!"

The consecration, or as it is commonly called, the "Baptism of the Bell," is conducted after an appropriate form of ceremonial, which may be found in the oldest Roman rituals extant. Meanwhile, the ceremony is not exactly baptismal, although

A Name Is Bestowed

on the bell in honor of some one of the saints, and certain persons who have been its donors, or who aid the church by pecuniary benefaction, are called its sponsors.

To return to St. Cecilia's. Very soon after three o'clock yesterday, the little church was crowded to its utmost capacity. The aisles and passages were filled with large numbers of men, standing, as was also the organ-gallery, while the vestry, and even the steps of the sanctuary itself were also invaded. We noticed in the audience a great many citizens from the Western District, and also

A Goodly Gathering

of non-Catholics, while the character of the assemblage was such as might be looked for in the heart of the city rather than at its bleak extremities. At the time mentioned, a procession of about sixty young girls, all dressed in white, came in by twos through the vestry, and took places at the front of the sanctuary. Their appearance was quite pretty and interesting, the younger children, from about four years to seven, being each crowned with a wreath of flowers, while those above that age wore the long white veil which is typical of girlish innocence and purity. Soon afterwards,

The Right Reverend Bishop

entered, being preceded by about twenty acolytes in red soutanes and white surplices, and also by the assistant priests in full canonicals. The latter consisted of Father M. G. Brennan, Deacon; Father M. Nevin, Master of Ceremonies; and Father Turner, Vicar-General of the Diocese. There were also in the sanctuary the Rev. Pastor, Father J. R. McDonald, pastor of St. Mary's Church; L'Abbe Aubrer, an Alsatian priest, now sojourning in this city, and Father Bobier.

Bishop Loughlin, robed in full pontificals and wearing his mitre, now ascended the altar steps, and crozier in hand, made

A Brief Address

to the congregation in reference to the ceremony which he was about to perform. He said that in conformity with the prescribed ritual the bell now before them was about to be dedicated to the service of the Church of God. It was to be used in this sacred edifice on certain occasions, and for certain purposes, but principally to summon those present to assemble for divine worship. It would also serve to remind them of the great mystery of the Incarnation, as in all Catholic countries it is rung in the morning, at noon, and in the evening at six o'clock, to unite the faithful in the recital of the *Angelus,* a beautiful form of prayer in which the Incarnation of the Son of God is proclaimed in the sentence "And the word was made flesh." In response to

This Glorious Intelligence,

which was the beginning of our redemption, the tones of the church bell should excite in every Christian heart the liveliest feelings of joy, sympathy and hope. Its office in thus recalling to them the mysteries of religion, is a most important and beneficent one. It would arouse them in the morning from their slumbers, to gather around the altar to praise and bless God, and to assist at the Holy Sacrifice of the Mass, which is the greatest act of homage that man can pay to his Creator. Then they could present their petitions to God and solicit His grace and blessing, by which alone salvation may be obtained. For no other purposes than these could the church bell be used, and because of its connection with them, it is now consecrated. The prayers to be said in this ceremony were

Not for the Material Bell,

which is nothing but inanimate matter, and could not be affected by them. The prayers were for the assembled people, petitioning God that they might be led to respond to its call, and regularly to perform those duties which would enable them to secure their eternal happiness. The Bishop concluded by a kindly reference to the donor, whose name he would not mention, and trusted that the congregation would remember him in their prayers. The venerable prelate then descended to the altar rail, in front of which the bell was placed within its wooden frame, and the ceremony of

The Benediction Began.

It was quite long and interesting, and opened with the reading of the fifty-third Psalm, after which the bell was asperged with holy water and incensed. Several other appropriate psalms followed, and then the formal prayer of benison was pronounced, whereby, in the name of the Holy Trinity, the bell in its various suggestive faculties and uses was dedicated forever to the service of God. The Bishop then laved the bell with water, inside and out, and dried it with towels, after which, like all the important utensils used in the Catholic Church, it was

Marked with Holy Oil,

or chrism, and once more incensed. Other psalms and prayers were then sung and said including the appropriate gospel, and the ceremony was at end. This Bishop soon after retired and the immense congregation dispersed, save and except the honorary sponsors, who, to the number twenty or thirty, adjourned to the pastoral residence close by.

A Pleasant Luncheon

was there partaken of and a contribution was made up for the support of the church. The modesty of some of the contributors precludes a mention of any of their names, but most of them were well-known citizens of the district.

The bell, we now learned, had been named Thomas, which is also the name of the large-hearted gentleman who presented it to the church. It is of

Handsome Form and Finish,

and is inscribed with the name of the founders and the year, it was cast by the celebrated firm of Jones & Co., of Troy, in this State, and this we know to be a sufficient guarantee of its excellent composition and sweetness of tone, the firm in question having furnished bells to nearly all the Catholic churches in these cities, including the one which was recently blessed in the Church of Saint Vincent de Paul in North Sixth Street.

We cannot withhold a word of eulogy in respect to the choral parts of yesterday's services, which were ably conducted by Dr. W. D. Fox, a gentleman who is indefatigable in the training of the youthful choir which he has in charge at St. Cecilia's.

N.B.—Thomas Riley, now deceased, was the donor of the bell.

It is a joy to add that the same bell, so solemnly blessed, is still performing its sacred duty, from the belfry of St. Anne's in Brentwood, Long Island, and it now calls worshippers to prayer.

First Resident Pastor.

In the year 1874, the Rev. Florence McCarthy was assigned to St. Cecelia's as first resident Pastor of the parish. Father McCarthy remained in charge until the year 1884. There was, during his pastorate, no regular parish Rectory, and we find Father McCarthy changing his dwelling place four times in the ten years. His last move proved most convenient of all for now he dwelt in Herbert Street within fifty feet of the Church. Wearing an illustrious Irish name, we may expect to find in the man strong Celtic traits. Father McCarthy could and did make heroic sacrifice in those hard early years of parish growth, but his nature could brook no interference and under the old Trustee System (now happily passed out of existence) lay interference in the material affairs of the Church was constantly arising. Lay members of the board of Trustees, mistaking a privilege for a right and the Pastor, knowing full well the exact difference between the two, friction was bound to arise, the more so there being no trace of diplomacy in Father McCarthy. Even the great Archbishop Hughes experienced trouble in destroying this false system of Church property control, a system hindering where it did not directly combat a fundamental right of pastoral authority. St. Cecilia's parish was the last one in Brooklyn to be freed from its humiliating and annoying influence. It was in vogue until about the fourth year of Father McGolrick's pastorate.

That the beginning years knew trials abundant is well shown by the following appeal, printed in tiny booklet form and issued to all families in the parish looking toward an increased membership in the Altar Society, which had been organized in May, 1874 by Father McCarthy.

ST. CECILIA ALTAR SOCIETY
Organized in May, 1874
Corner North Henry and Herbert Streets
Brooklyn, E. D.

DEAR FRIEND:

The object of this Society is to beautify and keep in order the Altar and its surroundings and to see that the Sanctuary, the little circle that Christ has marked out for himself in the church, will not be too unworthy of his presence. This society was organized by me in May 1874. About that time I commenced my mission here and finding the church entirely destitute of furniture. Immediately bought seven hundred dollars ($700) worth, on credit of Messrs. Benziger and Brothers, Broadway, N. Y. At the time of purchasing I hoped in a short time to be able to realize sufficient money from this society to pay the debt but failed owing to the few persons willing to be enrolled as members out of a very small congregation. The number enrolled in this society may be easily imagined when five dollars would average its monthly proceeds since its organization. This sum being bearly sufficient to keep two Priests daily in Altar wine, breads, tapers, incense and other incidental expenses during the month. Moreover the church being heavily mortgaged and the current expenses alone equal if not in excess of the income of the church made it impossible for me to cancel the entire debt before this. Hence why I am compelled to seek assistance in this way in order to pay a balance of a few hundred dollars yet due on church furniture. The initiation fee to the society will be fifty cents, monthly dues twenty-five cents. For all who in their charity help me in this matter I will say two masses everyweek for their intention whilst in this place and also they will share in the spiritual rewards accruing from three masses said every month for the members of the Rosary, Altar and Purgatorian Societies. The names of those wishing to become members and also bene-

factors will have their names written in this book, of the
collector's, and finally in a book religiously preserved in the
church as a voucher for those entitled to masses. Collectors
will make their returns one month after receiving their book
until the debt is paid, afterwards any time within three months.
No officers will preside over this society but the names of
collectors with the amount collected, also the names of contributors with the amount contributed will be published from
the Altar the first Sunday after the returns are all in. A statement of expenditure will also be given. Hoping thus to satisfy
all, and as the advantages of membership are great the burden
light and the object most dear to every Catholic heart, I expect
no one will refuse a little offering to pay off this debt. Recom-
mending bearer to your charity and begging most earnestly
your cooperation and assistance in this matter.

I remain very truly yours,

F. McCARTHY,
Pastor of St. Cecilia's.

There was also a distribution in book form of the Con-
stitution and By-Laws of St. Cecilia's Church Building Society,
organized by Father McCarthy in January of the year 1875.
The officers are given:

Florence McCarthy

Pastor, President, ex-officio, and Permanent Treasurer
Mathew Hart ....President
James McCabe ....Vice-President
John Glinnen ....Treasurer
Michael Gillespie ....Recording Secretary
Thomas Derrick ....Financial Secretary

An interesting statement of receipts and expenditures of
the parish, covering a period of seven years, was issued by
Father McCarthy in April, 1881. Viewed from this far day,
the report has an unusual attractiveness, not so much for its

facts of finance as for the larger thought it stirs in us. Perhaps not a single one whose name appears in this report is now alive. Our eyes fall upon the item "W. C. Bryant and Co. 1000 pamphlets." This, the very Bryant who entertained such serious thoughts on death while yet the blood of boyhood coursed through his veins. This, the historic figure in American literature, who wrote for us his deathless "Thanatopsis."

"The gay will laugh
When thou art gone, the solemn brood of care
Plod on, and each one as before will chase
His favorite phantom; yet all these shall leave
Their mirth and their employments, and shall come
And make their bed with thee."

This, the Bryant who, at nineteen, drew from his meditation on the universality of death, such wise counsel as Holy Mother the Church herself is forever giving:

"So live, that when thy summons comes to join
The innumerable caravan that moves
To the pale realms of shade, where each shall take
His chamber in the silent halls of death,
Thou go not, like the quarry slave at night,
Scourged to his dungeon, but, sustained and soothed
By an unfaltering trust, approach thy grave
Like one who wraps the drapery of his couch
About him, and lies down to pleasant dreams."

This statement furnishes proof that, from the very beginning, the people of St. Cecilia's parish were generous toward the helpless little ones, the orphans, and toward the suffering poor of that most Catholic land, Ireland. And this generosity so dear to the heart of St. Cecilia's present pastor, has ever been carefully nurtured by his spirit and example. It has doubtless drawn down upon priests and people heaven's blessing. The report follows:

Rev. F. McCarthy

In Account with
ST. CECILIA'S CHURCH
STATEMENT OF RECEIPTS AND EXPENDITURES
FOR SEVEN YEARS
From April 19th, 1874 to April 19th, 1881.
RECEIPTS

1874
SUNDAY

April	19,	Collections	$29.00
"	26,	"	25.00
May	3,	"	27.00
	10,	"	28.00
	17,	"	24.00
	24,	"	26.00
	31,	"	31.00
June	7,	"	28.00
	14,	"	30.00
	21,	"	27.00
	28,	"	31.00
July	5,	"	30.00
	12,	"	27.00
	19,	"	28.50
	26,	"	24.60
	14,	"	28.00
	21,	"	29.50
	28,	"	29.00
August	2,	"	28.20
	9,	"	29.00
	16,	"	27.00
	23,	"	31.00
	30,	"	29.00
September	6,	"	27.00
	13,	"	25.00
	20,	"	27.00
	27,	"	28.00
October	4,	"	28.00
	11,	"	29.00
	18,	"	29.00

	25,	"		27.00
November	1,	"		28.00
	8,	"		29.00
	15,	"		31.00
	22,	"		29.00
	29,	"		26.00
December	6,	"		24.00
	13,	"		25.00
	20,	"		24.00
	25,	"		130.00
	27,	"		24.00
		"	Total for 1874	$1150.30
1875				
January	3,	"		29.50
	10,	"		28.60
	17,	"		27.00
	24,	"		28.50
	31,	"		26.60
February	7,	"		28.00
	14,	"		29.00
	21,	"		28.60
	28,	"		29.00
March	7,	"		27.00
	14,	"		28.00
	21,	"		29.50
	28,	"		29.00
April	4,	"		28.00
	11,	"		29.00
	18,	"		27.50
	25,	"		31.00
May	2,	"		32.00
	9,	"		30.50
	16,	"		31.00
	23,	"		28.00
	30,	"		29.60
June	6,	"		31.00
	13,	"		30.50
	20,	"		31.00
	27,	"		30.50

July,	"		126.60
August,	"		156.00
September,	"		126.50
October,	"		154.50
November,	"		118.00
December,	"		242.50

Total for 1875	1682.00
Total for 1876	1812.95
Total for 1877	2068.05
Total for 1878	2223.70
Total for 1879	2286.87
Total for 1880	2401.25
Total for 1881	827.50

11620.32

Pew Rents for 1874, from June 7th	534.50
Pew Rents for 1875, from June 7th	731.25
Pew Rents for 1876, from June 7th	792.57
Pew Rents for 1877, from June 7th	723.50
Pew Rents for 1878, from June 7th	756.25
Pew Rents for 1879, from June 7th	668.00
Pew Rents for 1880, from June 7th	641.88
Pew Rents for 1881, from June 7th	163.00
*1874 Proceeds of Picnic at Boulevard Grove	700.00
1874 Proceeds of Excursion	975.00
1874 Received from Parishioners, to repair house	650.00

* The item of $700 credited as the proceeds of the Picnic in 1874 should read $250, as the balance was raised by my own personal exertions outside the Parish. Also, the item of $975, credited as the proceeds of the Excursion, in the same year, should read $300, as the balance was raised by myself, and added as in the case of the Picnic.

District Collections. From March 5, 1877, to Dec. 31, 1877	1053.74
From Jan. 9, 1878, to April 12, 1878	458.28
From April 20, 1878, to Aug. 10, 1878	493.52
From Aug. 17, 1878, to Nov. 30, 1878	381.55
From Nov. 30, 1878, to April 25, 1879	433.96
From May 7, 1879, to Sept. 13, 1879	379.38
From Sept. 20, 1879, to Feb. 1, 1880	437.31
From March 13, 1880, to Aug. 14, 1880	384.38

		From Sept. 9, 1880, to Jan. 27, 1881	422.61
		From Feb. 19, 1881, to May 11, 1881	335.00
		From May 1, 1875, to March 1, 1877	1250.00
		Rosary, Altar and Purgatorian Societies,	
		7 years	546.00
1875		Net Proceeds of two Picnics	550.00
		Net Proceeds of three Missions	900.00
1876		Net Proceeds of Picnic	230.00
1877		Net Proceeds of Picnic	225.00
September	2,	Contribution received by Mr. Fletcher for Flagging	12.50
		Net Proceeds of Concerts, Panoramas and Lectures,	
		for New Organ	564.00
October	7,	Received from Temperance Society	5.00
	21,	Received from Lecture by Fr. Williams	61.00
November	9,	Proceeds of Concert	45.00
1878			
April	18,	Collections for Orphans	110.00
June	16,	Collections for Yellow Fever Sufferers	60.00
August	7,	Net proceeds of Picnic	210.00
1879			
May	21,	Net proceeds of Picnic	190.00
1880			
March	28,	Collections for Orphans	100.00
June	28,	Net proceeds of Picnic	215.00
December	25,	Collections for Orphans	213.28
1881			
April	17,	Collections for Orphans	152.08
1876			
March	12,	Proceeds of Lecture	62.25
October	29,	Proceeds of Musical Vespers	63.00
March	11,	Proceeds of Lecture	80.00
		Collection for Paving and Grading	125.00
June	17,	Sacred Exhibition	44.56
		Net proceeds of Fair	1050.00

	$33,648.97
Sundry Receipts	674.04

Total Receipts for Seven Year................$34,323.01

EXPENDITURES.

1874

April	19,	James Nelson, services rendered to Church .... $	14.00
	20,	John Fell, Hardware	2.50
	22,	James Nelson, repairs on house	20.37
	23,	Thomas Penny, for stove pipe and putting up same	1.30
	24,	James McCreery, Serge for Altar	3.40
	24,	James Wilder & Co., Mdse.	20.95
	28,	Thomas Penny, three tin poor boxes	3.75
	28,	James Nelson, Paint, etc.	2.00
	29,	Sadlier & Co., Books for Sunday School Teachers	7.75
	30,	S. Woolsey, Carpets	31.50
		Gold chalice	40.00
		James McCabe and sister, as Organists	49.00
May	2,	John Sullivan, 300 tickets	1.50
	2,	Thomas Penny 16½ lbs. zinc.	2.97
	2,	Chris. Doyle, Mason, for plastering house	75.00
	2,	Charles Jansen, repairing priest's house	60.00
	4,	Costello, for painting fence	6.50
	6,	John Newman, cartage	1.00
	6,	J. & C. Dower, rail, newel and baluster	16.00
	8,	Thomas Mulhern, building fence	6.00
	8,	J. Dyer, white lead, putty, etc.	12.95
	8,	James Nelson, paints, oils, etc.	18.50
	8,	Thos. Mulhern, services to church	12.00
	10,	James Nelson, repairing house	10.84
	12,	Betts, heaters and stove	34.00
	16,	D. & J. Sadlier, small books for Sunday School teachers	5.50
	16,	Albrich, carpets	24.88
	18,	Charles O'Neil, carpenter work	20.00
	19,	Charles Jansen, carpenter work	246.56
	20,	J. Newshand, 5½ days labor	11.25
	20.	Chris. Doyle, masonry on house	100.00
	25,	Martin & Fell, hardware	39.00
	26,	Manahan's Band, 11 musicians	80.00
	28,	J. F. O'Neil, church music	6.00
	28,	S. Woolsey, carpets	15.12
	30,	Daniel Hickey, Masonry	12.00

	30,	O'Mahony, musical services as organist	24.00
	31,	Case for vestments	26.00
	31,	Repairing bell and rope	4.00
June	1,	S. Woolsey, Fixtures	2.05
	3,	H. Hemmeter, zinc, etc.	2.45
	5,	Thos. Mulhern, labor in cellar	2.00
	6,	Thos. Mulhern, brick	12.00
	6,	J. Brady, building closet	11.00
	6,	Painting inside of house	9.00
	5,	Thos. Mulhern, bricks, boards, etc.	4.00
	6,	M. Hickey, mason work	12.00
	13,	John Clark, oils and lamps	17.25
	13,	Thomas Mulhern, services to church	1.00
	13,	Michael Hickey, laying brick	12.00
	13,	Italian, per Thos. Mulhern, 2½ days of work	2.50
	13,	Thos. Mulhern, services to church	1.50
	13,	Thos. Mulhern, services to church	5.00
	15,	C. G. Covert, lime, lath and cement	13.20
	15,	Thos. Mulhern, lathing	1.12
	15,	C. G. Covert, lumber, shingles, etc.	74.63
	15,	G. Stone	20.30
	15,	Driscoll & Pritchard, crockery and glassware	92.40
	15,	M. Reilly, 43 feet steps	15.12
	17,	M. Hickey, 3000 bricks	10.50
	17,	M. Hickey, 12,000 bricks	36.00
	19,	M. Hickey, 12,000 bricks and 12 lb. nails	72.90
	19,	Thos. Mulhern, brick, sand and tank	30.50
	20,	John Sullivan, tickets, posters, etc.	27.50
	23,	George Stone, lumber	8.64
	26,	Fred Hindle, work in Priest's house	53.00
	26,	Charles Jansen, carpenter work	68.00
	28,	James Nelson, carpenter work	19.25
May	2,	Thos. Penny 1 tin poor box	2.00
July	1,	George Stone, lumber for fence	8.52
	1.	H. Hemmeter, for sheet iron	5.42
	10,	Thos. Brown, house painting	85.00
	11,	H. Hemmeter, work on church	5.42
	27,	W. C. Bryant, 100 cards	4.00
August	9,	Expenses of Sacred Concert	28.00
	17,	Peter Frank, music for picnic	60.00

	20,	Alexander Brown, seal press	1.00
	24,	E. H. Gerard, doors, windows, etc.	16.84
	24,	O. Mahoney, musical services as organist	8.00
	24,	Jas. Davis, 1000 excursion tickets	2.50
	19,	Jas. Davis, 3000 cards and 400 posters	25.00
September	1,	J. & T. Jones, lumber	21.16
	16,	Thos. Brown, paper, border, etc.	27.82
	31,	W. Eagan, 1000 orders of dance	9.00
November	4,	John Clark, chandeliers, etc.	16.15
December	26,	W. Green, Int. on bond and insurance	24.50
	30,	J. Mulhern, leader, solder, ¾ day-'s time	11.23

1875

January	31,	Jas. Reilly & Neil McMullen services	9.86
	17,	Benziger Bros., church furniture	5.00
February	9,	Richardson & Boynton, grate for stove, etc.,	4.60
	20,	W. C. Bryant & Co., 1000 pamphlets	20.00
	23,	John Schwartz, two insurance premiums	75.00
	23,	John Schwartz, interest on bond and mortgage	247.22
March	12,	Firmback for Organ	100.00
	12,	Cartage for Organ	3.00
April	18,	F. W. Parisette, altar wine	5.00
May	9,	Charles Jansen, handrail	16.00
	9,	Bryant & Co., 2000 tickets	6.00
	15,	W. Eagan, 4000 cards	11.00
	15,	John Sullivan, posters and orders of dance	11.50
June	9,	Golden, lumber and time	1.25
July	1,	Sammis & Bedford, carpenter work	225.68
	24,	J. Schwartz, interest on mortgage	227.50
	27,	M. P. O'Brien, Collection Books	7.40
August	1,	Sadlier & Co., for school books	50.19
	10,	Peter Frank, music	5.00
	12,	F. Steinhardt, hardware	.75
	17,	J. Schwartz, two premiums on insurance	75.00
	28,	W. J. Hamilton, 50 reports Fr. McDonald's acc'ts	10.50
September	11,	Benziger Bros., church ornaments	.75
October	3,	Keyser, 1 self-heater	18.00
	4,	Benziger Bros., Church furniture	502.55
	8,	Semanite & Miller, lamps	3.50
	31,	M. Purges, ventilators, pipes, etc.	26.40

November	3,	J. Schwartz, interest on bond and mortgage	227.50
	3,	Briem, Jr., as organist	10.00
	3,	Newman, stoves and pipe	24.00
	8,	John Clark, burners, chimneys, etc.	6.30
	15,	B. Fenton, 1 dozen blank books	2.00
December	4,	Benziger Bros., Church furniture	100.50
	4,	Edgar Darbee, pew receipts	7.50
	9,	H. C. Vaughan, chandeliers	12.75
	9,	H. C. Vaughan, chandeliers	19.40
	15,	N. Serf, 1 box candles	9.60
	20,	J. Hastings, labor 26 days at $1.50 per day	39.00
	23,	R. Kenyon, lumber and cartage	8.33
	24,	P. O'Shea, books, etc., for mission	180.63
	25,	Parisette Bros., altar wine	8.05
	29,	Semonite & Miller, station lantern	5.82
	31,	M. Purges, cleaning and repairing stoves	6.00
	31,	Fr. Rendoff, 3rd asst. on Christmas and Sunday	20.00
July	13,	Mortgage on lot North Henry Street	300.00
	13,	Interest on mortgage	15.75
	13,	Cost of Foreclosure	46.10
	13,	Satisfaction piece	2.00
1876			
January	1,	Moritz Hillig, lumber, hardware, etc.	72.54
	3,	J. Fell, hardware	3.43
	3,	R. Kenyon, shingles, lumber, etc., for school	210.25
	17,	C. Jansen, screen confessional	3.75
	28,	Sister Seraphin, for altar breads	18.00
February	3,	J. LeBrun, cards for pews	1.00
	4,	J. Hastings, services to church	66.00
	5,	Thos. Brown, house painting	28.98
	18,	J. Fell, hardware	19.88
	22,	John Kelly, 1500 tickets	3.75
March	1,	G. W. Devoe, cleaning water pipe	1.25
	21,	Kenyon, lumber	3.45
	29,	Kenyon, lumber for building desks	211.00
	27,	James Kirwin, carpenter work for school	34.50
	27,	Walter Klots, brick, lime, etc.	1.95
	29,	Walter Klots, brick, lime, etc.	1.20
	29,	Daniel Hickey, mason work	8.00
April	21,	Collection, orphans (sent to Bishop)	100.00

	21,	Parisette, altar wine	11.90
	21,	W. E. McTighe, as member of the committee to examine Rev. J. R. McDonald's accounts	20.00
	21,	J. Glinnon, services to church	25.00
May	6,	J. C. Durfee, muslin for altar	1.24
	17,	M. Wells, cartage	1.50
	24,	Newman, lumber	2.75
	24,	Peter Frank, Music for picnic	66.00
	25,	H. Bopp, white roses, gold tassels, for picnic	5.30
June	7,	Saddler & Son	15.00
	9,	Parisette, altar wine	13.45
	30,	P. O'Shea, books, etc., for school	70.00
July	1,	R. W. Kenyon, lumber	3.45
September	9,	J. Le Brun, 300 vesper tickets	1.50
October	27,	J. Glennon, services to St. Cecilia's Church	12.50
November	5,	J. Glennon, services to St. Cecilia's Church	22.50
	13,	M. Purges, for tin work	4.20
	18,	J. L. Peters, Willard's Mass in G.	3.75
	21,	Mrs. McCabe, music	3.75
	27,	J. Newman, cleaning stove and pipe	11.00
December	3,	Parisette altar wine	24.00
	3,	Cleaning school house	8.00
	3,	Building fire in school house	14.00
	12,	R. W. Kenyon, lumber	3.00
	12,	New Fireboard	3.00
	25,	Lazarists Priests, Christmas services	15.00
1877			
January	1,	Repairing roof on vestry spire	15.00
	8,	J. Newman, stove	4.00
	8,	Coal Scuttle	1.80
February	1,	Sammis & Bedford, carpenter work	1.50
	1,	Smith & Crane, altar	100.00
	1,	M. Purges, roof repairing	6.15
	1,	M. Purges, repairing	1.95
	10,	Jacob Mersmer, nails, screws, etc.	6.12
	18,	C. Meyer, 6 months interest on mortgage	299.62
	18,	Lot on North Henry Street on account	600.00
	18,	Cleaning school	1.80
	18,	C. Meyer, purchase money St. Cecilia's Church	1000.00
	18,	Hockmeyer, drawing up deeds, of church	25.00

	24,	Kings County Fire Insurance Co.	25.00
	24,	Farragut Fire Insurance Co.	25.00
	26,	F. Meinhardt, repairing bell	.70
February	26,	Locks and Keys for poor boxes and church	50.00
	26,	Mrs. McCabe, Musical services to church	3.00
	26,	J. Peters, church music	21.41
March	5,	Geo. L. Fox, premium on insurance	50.00
	5,	Geo. L. Fox, putting deed on record	2.00
	10,	J. A. Boynton, repairing furnace	25.00
	10,	M. Purges, balance for roof repairs	4.65
	12,	K. McCanna teaching school	80.00
	19,	Parisette, altar wines	9.10
	27,	Newman, lumber	1.57
April	20,	P. H. Murray, flagging North Henry Street	100.00
May	11,	Moritz Hillig, repairing matting	5.75
	15,	Richardson, photographs of church	15.00
June	4,	C. Murphy, altar wine	3.75
	14,	John Sullivan, 2000 tickets and 300 posters	14.00
July	1,	J. Glenning, services to church	11.00
	1,	Clearing in front of church	18.00
	1,	P. Foley, teaching school	200.00
	2,	P. O'Shea, school books	200.19
	2,	Attorney Rogers, services to church	50.00
	25,	M. King, 1000 pamphlets	4.50
August	17,	Benziger Bros., church furniture	5.00
	17,	Gordon & Sons, music	2.04
	18,	C. Meyer, interest on bond and mortgage	209.63
	20,	Roosey & Co., choir books	1.35
	20,	Ditson & Co., music	.60
September	1,	Sammins & Bedford, carpenter work on church	66.00
October	3,	P. O'Shea, school books	150.00
	3,	Chas. Bogan, insurance premium	25.00
	29,	P. Mulhern, sodding in front of Church	15.00
November	9,	Tinning spire on Church	12.00
	12,	J. Le Brun, tickets, posters, etc.	12.00
	19,	J. Newman, pipe repairing	21.50
	26,	P. O'Shea, school books	25.00
	30,	J. Clark, lamps burners, etc.	9.87
December	5,	Sammis & Bedford, tin work on church	15.00
	6,	P. O'Shea, School books	227.31

	6,	P. O'Shea, School books	100.00
	28,	Fr. Hannigan, assistant on Christmas	16.00
	31,	P. Murray, flagging Herbert Street	200.00
1878			
January	1,	Parisette, altar wines	9.40
	1,	Parisette, altar wines	7.50
	2,	F. Pustet, two poor boxes	12.00
February	18,	C. Meyer, interest on mortgage	299.63
	24,	Kings County Fire Insurance Co.	25.00
	24,	Farragut Fire Insurance Co.	25.00
	26,	James Tashler, repairing lamps	9.00
March	17,	Choir, for solemn high mass of requiem, for Pope Piux IX.	25.00
	18,	P. O'Shea, books for school	61.50
	27,	Grading and paving North Henry Street	58.57
	27,	Grading and paving North Henry Street	234.27
April	18,	Collections for Orphans (sent to Bishop)	110.00
	29,	G. L. Fox, drawing up deed of lot in N. Henry St. in bishop's name	6.50
	29,	Firmback, repairing organ and melodion	40.00
May	13,	Pictures for altar boys	5.00
	13,	Briem, Jr., as organist	12.00
	13,	Music for church	2.50
	13,	Mrs. Hoey, teaching choir	5.75
	13,	J. Nelson, building closet in Frost Street	7.50
June	1,	Parisette, altar wine	11.65
	8,	M. King, printing	4.75
	16,	Collection for Pope (sent to Bishop)	40.00
	24,	M. King, 200 posters	5.50
	24,	J. Dawekins, Mirror exhibition	55.00
	25,	M. King, 2000 picnic tickets	3.75
	27,	Thomas Brown, painting church	200.00
July	20,	Ditson & Co, music	5.20
August	7,	Glany & Schmid High Ground Park, for picnic	30.00
	11,	Mrs. Hoey, teaching choir	7.00
	11,	Confessional Stole	3.75
	23,	Parisette, altar wine	6.25
September	20,	Collection for Yellow Fever sufferers	60.00
	21,	K. Hart, altar furniture	1.50
	21,	Striker for gong	1.00

	21,	Mrs. Hoey, singing teacher for choir	2.00
	21,	Repairing Chandelier	4.50
	26,	Attorney Rogers, fee for services to church	25.00
October	14,	Chandeliers in Gallery	4.00
November	5,	Jos. McKee's Sons, heater, pipe, etc.	15.25
	10,	J. M. Peterson, cartage and use of piano	6.00
	15,	Repairing Vestments	3.00
	25,	P. O'Shea, mission books	86.63
December	19,	Grading and Paving Herbert Street	190.12
	20,	J. Corbett, lamps, etc., for church	6.00
	22,	Semonite & Miller Bros., burners, etc.	.67
	23,	P. O'Shea, school books	2.79
	25,	Collections for orphans (sent to Bishop)	142.12
1879			
January	16,	Repairing Organ	3.00
	28,	New Grate for furnace	10.00
	28,	New Zinc in Spire	8.50
February	24,	John Fox, insurance premium	50.00
	24,	C. Meyer, interest on bond and mortgage	299.63
	24,	On account of Mortgage	520.00
March	28,	Collections for orphans (sent to Bishop)	110.00
	29,	Repairing Cross on Banner	1.50
April	21,	M. Doyle, organist	10.00
	23,	Removing furniture	5.30
May	3,	Sammis & Bedford, book case	14.50
	6,	Repairing Osten Sorium	13.25
	15,	Thomas Brown, paper border	3.04
	31,	D. C. Hayes, 500 posters	8.00
	31,	Parisette & Co., altar wine	1.25
June	1,	Sammis & Bedford, nails, lumber, etc.	24.39
	6,	Repairing church windows	.98
	16,	M. King, 1000 orders of dance and tassels	6.50
	21,	J. D., Barton, 4 cars from Humboldt Street to Myrtle Avenue park	30.00
	30,	Repairing Cross	4.00
July	1,	Parisette, altar wine	2.50
	3,	Sammis & Bedford, lumber	24.39
	13,	J. D. Barton, 2 cars for picnic	10.00
	26,	N. Y. Job Printing Co., book of receipts	5.00

August	19,	C. Meyer, interest on bond and mortgage	282.14
	25,	Benziger Bros., Incense	4.50
September	19,	Mrs. Lace, materials for surplice and albs.	12.00
	25,	Charles Linchauer, candle sticks	27.00
October	10,	P. O'Shea, books for mission	182.75
	15,	Parisette, altar wine	5.15
	15,	J. Glinnen, 100 children's tickets	5.30
	25,	Pictures for children	7.28
November	1,	Christian Gabriel, grate, pipe, etc.	11.00
	17,	M. King, 2000 temperance pledges	14.00
	17,	Richardson, Boynton & Co., repairs to furnaces	49.00
	17,	Repairs to chandeliers	4.00
	25,	Gave Newman for services rendered to Church two stoves presented by Deputy Sheriff Murphy of New York, and worth	30.00
December	14,	For O'Leary, 5 weeks services as 3rd assistant	25.00
	17,	Saulter for coach to college for Priest	3.00
	23,	Lamps for Church	5.00
	25,	Collection for orphans sent to Bishop	145.00

1880

January	10,	Parisette, altar wines	5.00
February	1,	For O'Leary	5.30
	1,	Collection for Ireland	140.00
	19,	C. Meyer, interest on mortgage and part on account	782.14
	21,	Geo. Gardine, 1st instalment on organ	300.00
	24,	Kings County Fire Insurance Co.	25.00
	24,	Farragut Fire Insurance Co.	25.00
March	7,	Music	10.00
	9,	Music	3.00
	10,	Sammis & Bedford, platform for organ and case for music	13.00
	11,	Taylor & Son, 100 Florida palm leaves	7.00
	27,	D. & J. Saddlier, hymn books	13.00
	28,	Collection for orphans, sent to Bishop	110.00
April	1,	Thomas Doyle, roofing tower on Church	11.00
	4,	A. McCauly, blowing organ	2.00
	17,	M. Connel, music	3.67
	22,	M. Connell, music	.29
May	3,	A. McCauly, blowing organ	2.00
	3,	K. Hart, altar furniture	2.00

	3,	Vessel for holy water	1.25
	3,	Flowers	4.00
	13,	G. B. Horton, plumbing	11.25
	20,	D. C. Hayes, tickets and posters	14,00
June	1,	Geo. Jardine, on account of organ	50.00
	13,	A. McCauley, blowing organ	3.00
	19,	D. C. Hayes, printing	9.00
	22,	J. D. Barton, 6 picnic cars to Myrtle Avenue park	30.00
	27,	A. McCauley, blowing organ	2.00
August	20,	C. Meyer, interest on mortgage	264.64
	29,	A. McCauley, blowing organ	2.00
September	3,	Geo. Jardine, on account for organ	25.00
October	3,	Supper for members of choir, singing at concert	13.00
	13,	Geo. Jardine, on account for organ	55.00
November	5,	Repairing pipe of furnace and new stoves	21.00
	9,	Self-Heater for house	10.75
	16,	Geo. Jardine, on account of organ	34.00
	18,	E. Sutphin, pipe, joints, elbows, etc.	21.99
	20,	Photographs for Fair	16.96
	24,	Mechanical Organette Co., organette for Fair	8.06
December	25,	Collection for orphans (sent to Bishop)	231.28
1881			
January	3,	Lewis, two frames for fair, one of which was stolen	3.15
	3,	Reynolds, coal	5.75
	13,	E. Sutphin, repairing roof	1.50
	29,	Jos. McKees's Sons, grate, fire pot, etc.	3.75
February	19,	C. Meyer, interest on mortgage, part on account	764.63
	19,	Farragut Fire Insurance Co., premium	25.00
	19,	Kings County Fire Insurance Co., premium	25.00
	25,	Higgins, Tooker & Co., collection books	1.80
April	17,	Collections for orphans (sent to Bishop)	152.08
		Palm for six Easter Sundays	64.00
		7 Easter Candles at $5 each	35.00
		House Rent, J. Nelson's house $255; Speers $500	755.00
		Ice for seven years	70.00
		Kerosene Oil, seven years at $50 per year	350.00
		Cleaning Church, seven years	470.00
		Fixing Windows, seven years at $5 per year	35.00
		Putting up stoves, seven years, at $20 per year	140.00
		Gong for Church	33.00

Attorney Rogers, services to church	10.00
Ex. U. S. District Attorney, Courtney, services to church	50.00
Attorney Rogers, services to church	5.00
Decorating church at Christmas, with wreaths and trees, 6 years	60.00
Repairing school house	350.00
Altar bread, 7 years at $19 per year	133.00
M. Doyle, 2 years services as organist	80.00
*Incidental Expenses	7896.00
Repositories for Easter Sunday, 7 years	49.00
Tapers for Church, 7 years	12.00
Incense for Church, 7 years	42.06
Charcoal for Church, 7 years	65.20
Running errands for Church, 7 years	84.00
Matting for Church	50.00
Curtains for Confessional	4.00
2000 Church Building Society Books	20.00

1874
May   28,   Mrs. Lewis & Gorman, cleaning church and house   17.00

1874
August   10,   John Kennedy, grading yard   6.00

Mr. Riley, digging closet 10 feet deep, in rear of church	7.00
Building closet rear of church	12.00
P. C. Ingersoll, chairs and camp stools for sanctuary	15.00
Paper for flower pots, for Blessed Virgin's altar	2.23
Salary paid to assistant Pastor, $600 a year for 7 years	4200.00
Miscellaneous accounts too numerous to itemize, vouchers for which can be shown	1872.37

Total, $33,334.78

* The item of incidental expenses may seem excessive, but it must be remembered that wages paid to domestics, household expenses and furniture, which would amount to nearly double the item of incidental expenses, are not included in this statement.

BONDED DEBT.

On church $7061.14

FLOATING DEBT.

On organ ....$ 86.00

Salary due Pastor 5600.00

Cash in Bank in account with church.. $ 988.23

For all the items contained in this report, vouchers will be shown to tally with each one; also to account for the correctness of incidental expenses.

Most respectfully submitted,

F. McCarthy.

We have examined these accounts
and find them correct.

D. C. Hayes,

Jas. Shaughnessy.

FATHER MALONE TAKES CHARGE.

Father Michael Malone became acting pastor of St. Cecilia's
in 1884 and continued in charge until November 9, 1888, when
failing health necessitated his retirement. Throughout Father
Malone's four years of service to the parish, he occupied the
little dwelling next door to the then existing frame church.
This dwelling had been purchased in Father McCarthy's time,
but on it, as well as on the church, rested a heavy mortgage.

Other than Church records, baptisms, marriages, etc. we
have only a printed Financial Statement for the year ending
April 21, 1886, during Father Malone's pastorate. This report
is here given:

FINANCIAL REPORT

—— of ——

ST. CECILIA'S CHURCH

Brooklyn, E. D.

From April 21st, 1885 to April 21st, 1886.

RECEIPTS

Door and Plate Collections	$4604.17
Pew Rent	428.25
Collection for the Holy Father	65.48
Collection for the Seminarians	81.80
Collection for Orphans, Christmas	210.56
Altar Society	165.30
Rosary Society	44.62
Donations	22.48
Loan of Pastor	251.88
Total	$5874.54
Expenses	5761.28
Balance on hand	$ 113.26

PRESENT DEBTS

Mortgage on Church	$5561.00
Mortgage on House	1400.00
Loan to Church by Pastor	251.88
Benziger Bros.	226.00
Schulz	112.37
Total	$7551.25

EXPENSES

Altar Expenses	$ 196.81
Priests' Salaries	1600.00
Music and Printing	40.33
House Rent, 4 months	120.00
Taxes and arrears of Taxes	626.82
Organist	200.00
Plumbing	247.30
Care of Church and Repairing Windows	209.00
Painting Church and House	265.49
Interest on Church Mortgage, C. Meyer	333.66
M. O'Grady's Note and Interest	560.00
Interest on House, A. Wyman	27.00
Stoves and Tin Work	20.55
Mason Work, C. Doyle	95.15
Gas and Coal	162.55
Flagging, Jackson	86.00
Holy Father	65.48
Seminarians	81.80
Orphans, Christmas	210.56
Schultz	172.59
Sammis & Bedford	127.54
Benzinger	100.00
Carpenter Work, Carolan	177.00
Sundries	35.65
Total	$5761.28

M. J. MALONE, *Rector.*

PRESENT PASTOR APPOINTED.

The appointment of Father Edward J. McGolrick as pastor of the parish went into effect on November 9, 1888, when the young priest arrived in time to hear the Saturday confessions. The day and the dwelling were cheerless but Father Malone awaited his coming and gave him kindly welcome,—a welcome which lives in grateful memory in the heart of the present Monsignor McGolrick.

What picture presented itself to Father McGolrick on that November day can best be imagined from a brief, forceful description, appearing in a letter written from St. Patrick's Rectory thirteen years later by the Rev. Wm. J. White, D. D. As a boy, Rev. Doctor White had taken Latin lessons from Father McGolrick who was then stationed as a curate at St. Patrick's. From the letter, written on the occasion of the consecration of St. Cecilia's Church one reads:

"Tempora mutantur! I was one of the first to visit you in your new parish. You left St. Patrick's, ni fallor, on Saturday and I went over to St. Cecilia's on Sunday. *What a collection of barns you had then!* The memory of your struggles and triumph will help us youngsters. We needn't go back to ancient or medieval history for ideals. With warmest congratulations."

Father McGolrick's naturally buoyant and as naturally religious nature shut out discouragement. Every moment of his time was needed now, not for self pity but for the great work there was to do, that is, the caring for the spiritual life of his people and the temporal needs of the parish.

In May, 1889, he took up his first house to house collection, —receiving from a warmhearted and sincere people the grand total of three thousand one hundred thirty-five dollars and seventy cents. Immediately, a printed statement was issued, photographic copy of which is here given. Time has frayed the pages, denying this book the inclusion of some few names and amounts. What matter! St. Cecilia's was then, as it is now, a congregation made up in general of the toiling classes. In nearly every instance a donation to the Church meant sacrifice. The donors gave not for any temporal glory nor for the return of human gratitude. Their faith was sure; their love of God fervent; their sacrifices are one and all writ in the unfrayable records of God.

CENSUS COLLECTION
MAY 1889

St. Cecilia's Roman Catholic Church,
Brooklyn, N. Y.

Herbert St.

Kingsland Ave.

Wilber St.

Jackson St.

Leonard St.

Leonard St.

Manhattan Ave.

Eckford St.

Oakland St.

Newel St.

Diamond St.

Ewen St.

Meeker Ave.

Bedford Ave.

Vancott Ave.

Meeker Ave. and Penny Bridge

Morgan Ave.

Meeker Ave.

Spring Terrace.

Lombardi St.

Bennet St.

Benton St.

Russell St.

Bayard St.

Nassau Ave.

Broome St.

Parker St.

Banzett St.

Maspeth Ave.

Herbert St.

Humboldt St.

Humboldt St.

North Henry St.

Division Place

TOTAL BY STREETS, OR SUMMARY.

This collection speaks most eloquently for the Faith and Charity of the people of St. Cecilia's. Not one dollar was sought beyond the limits of the Parish. We sincerely think those whose names are on this list, and many others whose circumstances would not permit them doing what their hearts dictated, Yet the kind manner in which we though comparatively unknown, were received by them in their homes.

EDWARD J. McCORMICK, Rector St. Cecilia's.

Brooklyn, May 15, 1889.

D. P. MURPHY, Jr., Church Stationer, 64 Vesey St., New York.

ANNUAL CENSUS NEVER OMITTED.

The annual census of the parish has never been omitted through the forty-two years of Father McGolrick's pastorate. Thus has he ever remained in close touch with all of his people.

The new pastor, eager for building funds, appointed a number of young men as weekly street collectors, i.e., who would collect from Catholic families each week in the street or streets assigned them. This plan proved most successful.

The subjoined report shows the substantial amount gathered by these young men for the year ending April 21, 1892.

An interesting item also is the one designated—"Proceeds from the Drawing of Horse and Carriage" in that it reminds us how recent the introduction of the auto. And there is another item called "Restitution." No name, no earthly glory goes with such donation. It is a matter resting solely with God and the individual soul. How grand and comforting the Faith that so connects Heaven with Earth, the Creator with the creature; that places little value on man's opinion but forever emphasizes God's certain knowledge; that teaches not seeming, but being. Not that man shall think you honest but that God shall know you so is the burden of Catholic teaching. Police courts may flourish and may fade, but the tribunals of justice in the Church of Christ go silently, patiently, steadily on with their purging work through all the centuries since our Lord established them. An inspiring lesson for us all on the power and efficacy of the Grand Old Faith is that one small item "Restitution."

FINANCIAL STATEMENT
—— of ——
ST. CECILIA'S ROMAN CATHOLIC CHURCH
Brooklyn, E. D.

For the Fiscal Year ending April 21st, 1892.

RECEIPTS

Balance on hand, April 21, 1891	$22,444.09
Weekly Street Collections	5,187.12
Seat and Plate Collection	8,944.64
Pew-Rent	691.00
Interest on Money	321.32
Donation of Herbert Council	323.06
House Sold	200.00
Cornerstone Collection	1,143.65
St. Aloysius Sodality	141.56
To be added to Annual Collection of Last Year	105.70
Proceeds from Drawing for Horse and Carriage	1,419.00
Sodality of B. V. Mary	67.00
Children's Brick-Books	651.00
Sale of Pictures of Church	36.00
St. Patrick's Day Lecture	25.00
Sale of Stone	11.50
Young Men's Picnic	12.00
Collection for Bell	30.77
Restitution	20.00
Mr. Hennessy, Contractor on Foundation	20.00
A Friend	50.00
Mr. Deitjen	25.00
Mr. D. Herbert	53.00
House Rent	10.00
Mr. Whitmann	10.00
Mr. Wm. Lavin	5.00
Iron Workers on New Church	11.00
Collection for Seminarians	60.00
Collection for Holy Father	40.63
Collection for Holy Land	4.00

$42,062.04

EXPENDITURES

Pastor's and Assistant's Salary	$ 2,000.00
Sexton	388.00
Extra Priests Services	13.00
Coal and Gas	178.79
Insurance, Water and City Taxes	239.44
Choir Expenses	405.52
Legal Expenses	104.70
T. H. Poole, Architect	1,300.00
Byrne & Perry, Builders	25,500.00
Moving Church	1,108.37
Household Goods	64.91
Hardware and Repairs	120.81
Steam Heating (Old Church)	493.00
Lithographs of New Church	55.00
Donation to Sisters	50.00
Prizes	99.55
Printing	127.75
Repairing Windows and Plumbing	115.19
Lumber for Tower	17.23
Appurtances for Bell	40.00
Palm and Christmas Decorations	16.00
Paid Rt. Rev. Bishop for Indians and Negroes	37.00
Paid Rt. Rev. Bishop for Holy Land	4.00
Paid Rt. Rev. Bishop for Clerical Relief Fund	20.00
Paid Rt. Rev. Bishop for Holy Father	40.63
Paid Rt. Rev. Bishop for Seminarians	60.00
	$32,598.89

Leaving in the Treasury a balance of Nine Thousand Four Hundred and Sixty-three Dollars and fifteen cents ($9,463.15).

EDWARD J. McGOLRICK, *Rector.*

ST. CECILIA'S CHURCH.

In January, 1891 the energetic young pastor started forth on a rather hard errand. He made his way direct to Bishop Loughlin's residence, and before his courage could fail him he began—

"Bishop, I don't think it's worthwhile adding to that Church!"

"You don't, why not?"

"Well, it's old, and small, and a frame building, subject to fire's havoc—"

"What would a new church cost?"

"I might build one for $150,000."

"What did St. Patrick's cost?"

"About $45,000."

"And you are thinking of a hundred fifty thousand dollar church! Why, how could you attempt that?"

"Well, Bishop, I've been at St. Cecilia's two years and two months. In that time, I've given out two yearly statements showing that the parish has raised over forty thousand dollars."

"Go home," said the Bishop, "and do what you like!"

There was nor worry for Father McGolrick on that homeward journey. All the world was filled with hope and joy and promise!

This the beginning of the present magnificent edifice of St. Cecilia's. From frame to marble the pastor's thoughts took leap. He called the representatives of the parish together and discussed with them the type of church that section needed. A frame church was hazardous all agreed, but a brick church seemed to be in general favor. The Pastor's nature was not one that would blindly follow a majority, right or wrong, neither was it one that could wantonly dominate or antagonize.

Father McGolrick had looked with wonder and admiration upon the magnificent pre-"reformation" Cathedrals of Ireland,

RT. REV. JOHN LOUGHLIN, D. D.
First Bishop of Brooklyn

still standing in all their architectural beauty, solemnly testi-
fying unto the centuries, despite intervening robbery and
calumny, to the religious zeal and esthetic culture of the
Catholic Gaels who builded them. He had looked upon
London's ancient and ever beautiful Benedictine Abbey, which,
notwithstanding its altered use, still speaks of the monks who
planned its beauty, of the faithful who in ages gone were
buried there, of Catholicism that was in England when King
by Pope was knighted its "Defender." He had had through
Seminary life in the central city of all Christendom excellent
opportunity to consider the endurance and abiding beauty of
the Houses of Worship built in early ages when all talent,
all genius was directed toward them. He had been ordained
in Rome's overwhelmingly beautiful basilica of the Lateran.
It was then his task to inspire his people with a whole-hearted
desire to erect the right kind of Church. In his heart dwelt
inherent culture and certain knowledge and from his tongue
flamed Celtic eloquence. Such combination soon induced a-
mong the members of that meeting a loyal agreement, a whole-
hearted, unanimous motion for the type of Church their Pastor
visioned. It stands today in all its enduring beauty at the
summit spot of the neighborhood, the intersection of Herbert
and North Henry Streets.

Father McGolrick brought to Thomas H. Poole, the architect, no hazy half-formed notions. The Church architecture he
desired must embody the art of building beautifully and
expressively and, at the same time, of subordinating means to
ends, making sure that the primary end was never superceded.
He desired Brooklyn's St. Cecilia's to be a thing of beauty
but a beauty subservient to the sense of fitness. It must not
merely satisfy the eye of the artist, not merely please the
passerby. No, the building which Father McGolrick demanded
must be one suited to public Catholic worship—it must meet

the needs of the faithful who were to worship within its walls, and it must also be in itself an expression of an act of worshipful homage to the God of love and truth and beauty. His choice naturally turned toward the Basilica type of edifice—the Romanesque—for with that he was most familiar.

The Basilica or Romanesque Church has a central nave flanked with aisles and lighted by clear-story fenestration. The window heads are arched in correspondence with the successive arched recesses constituting what we commonly call the side aisles. The elevated, and usually semi-circular, extention at the Eastern end of the nave is called the apse. In early times, the apse opened directly into the nave. Later, there was a cross-section or transept interposed to give greater space in the central part of the building for the location of the Canon's choir. This oblong hall extended beyond the aisles and not only gave additional space but lent a symbolism to the formation of the church. Later still, a projecting chancel was built, forming a fourth limb to the cross — a crux commissa — as it is designated in church architecture. It is this form of Romanesque we find in St. Cecilia's, bestowing itself adequately to the many solemn and beautiful ceremonies which take place within this sacred edifice.

The High Altar is apsidal. Three steps lead from the Sanctuary floor to its predella, and the lower front of the altar shows a bas-relief carving of Angels presenting the chalice to the Eternal Father. The decorative reredos rises high above the gradini at the back of the altar. At either side, above the ornation of the cornice of the reredos, stands a trumpeting angel.

The lofty summit of the ciborium-like superstructure of the tabernacle is surmounted by the cross. This dignified and beautiful architectural treatment draws the eye of the worshipper to the altar's Central Fact—the Real Presence—. For

HIM was all this designed —for HIM who is our Friend in want and sorrow, our Friend in the hour of pleasure's lure—our Friend in health and sickness—our Friend who alone of all we hold dear will accompany us on the dreaded journey of death—our Friend who is to be our Judge—our Friend who was so loved by Saint Cecilia, the virgin saint to whom the parish is dedicated, that she gladly laid down her young life in His honor. All the beauty of Thy house, O Lord, is for Thee without those Presence St. Cecilia's would be a lonesome place.

On either side of the Sanctuary beautifully carved lattice work acts as extention to the reredos in imitation of the older altar screen. Arched openings therein lead behind the altar.

Appearing to flank each chancel wall and framed by the lesser arches adjacent to the central terminal one, are the altars dedicated to the Blessed Virgin and to her spouse, St. Joseph. In reality, these altars are isolated. Behind each, and well out from the chancel wall, is built a lattice work which acts as reredos to the altar and at the same time forms a passageway to the Sacristy.

Along the vaulted nave, transept arms and chancel walls runs a simulatory gallery which gives a very pleasing disposition to the wall space between arch-tops and clear-story windows. Simulant entrances to this gallery appear on either side of the transept windows.

The square tower erected at the Herbert-North Henry corner of the building, bestows on St. Cecelia's a commanding elevation. There is an artistic colonnaded ambulatory leading from the adjoining Rectory along the baptistry to the transept extension of the edifice. This architectural effect augments the beauty of the exterior, lending to the exposed Herbert Street facade a remarkably correct and pleasing unity, including, as it does, the Rectory corresponding in material and design.

When the architect's plans were approved, building bids were offered and the firm of Byrne and Perry secured the contract.

The corner-stone was laid September 27, 1891, by Bishop Loughlin.

Emerson, in his work on "Society and Solitude," writes: "The Gothic Cathedrals were built when builder and priest and people were overpowered by their faith." Emerson was never more mistaken. He should have written: 'The Gothic Cathedrals were built when builder and priest and people were *em*powered by their faith.'

Thus, down the centuries will the white marble edifice brightening with the years be standing witness to the *em*powering of faith in builder and priest and people. How zealously did all labor together that an enduring edifice for Christian worship might raise its heavenward tower in their midst; that fitting abode for the Holy of Holies might be erected among them; that their own hearts might within its sacred walls feel the unequalled peace growing out of close communion with His Tabernacled Presence.

Mr. Bentley, architect for the new Westminster Cathedral in London, said at a dinner tendered him some years ago in St. Francis College, New York City, that he considered St. Cecelia's in Brooklyn one of the very finest speciments of church architecture he had seen in America. When one reflects on the genius of Bentley, on the type of church building he has given to present-day England, such compliment to the church in Brooklyn takes on a worthwhile value.

Souvenir of Consecration.

Facts concerning the foundation and history of St. Cecelia's Church are briefly given in the subjoined "Souvenir of Consecration" edited by the Pastor and distributed among the people on Sunday, November 24, 1901, the Sunday within the octave of the Feast of the titular saint of the parish.

ST. CECELIA'S R. C. CHURCH

With joy we behold it, a vision of beauty!
An edifice fitting for sanctity's home.

—Sr. of St. Joseph.

(a former parishioner.)

MEMORABILIA.

The corner-stone was laid on the 27th of September, 1891, by the Rt. Rev. John Loughlin, first Bishop of Brooklyn.

The dimensions of the Church are 90 feet by 165 feet; transept, 100 feet in width.

Style of architecture is Romanesque.

Seating capacity is 1,400.

The Church was finished in two years and dedicated on the 26th of November, 1893, by the Rt. Rev. Charles E. McDonnel, Bishop of the Diocese.

The Solemn Pontifical Mass on that occasion was celebrated by His Excellency Archbishop Francis Satolli, first Apostolic Delegate to the United States, now Cardinal of the Holy Roman Church.

The Dedicatory Sermon was delivered by the Rev. Thomas J. Shahan, of the Catholic University, Washington, D. C.

The total cost of Church, Chapel and Rectory was about $200,-000.00.

During the past five years we have cleared off the mortgage of $60,000.00.

Our Church was consecrated yesterday, November 23rd, by our Rt. Rev. Bishop McDonnell.

We return thanks to Almighty God, to His Blessed Mother, Mary, to our patron, St. Cecelia, to the people of our parish, and to all those who in any way helped to make possible this day of joy and triumph.

EDWARD J. McGOLRICK,
Rector of St. Cecilia's.

RT. REV. CHARLES E. McDONNELL
Second Bishop of Brooklyn

UNITED EFFORT.

How unitedly priests and people worked together for the eradication of the debt upon their new and beautiful edifice is made manifest in the financial statement of the year 1901, the year in which St. Cecelia's was consecrated.

FINANCIAL STATEMENT
—— of ——
PAROCHIAL VISITATIONS
ST. CECILIA'S R. C. CHURCH, 1901.

Rev. Edward J. McGolrick	$500.00
Mr Edward Gibney	500.00
In Memoriam, Dr. G. W. Delap	100.00
Messrs. M. Fogarty & Bro.	50.00
Mrs. Clarkson	25.00
Mr. George Gerrity, Corona, L. I.	10.00
Mr. Louis Hannweber	10.00
St. Aloysius Sodality	50.00
St. Cecilia Council, C. W. B. L.	100.00
Mrs. Mary Carey	50.00

Humboldt Street

Myles Ward	$5.00
John Bedell	1.00
Philip Quirk	1.00
Mr. Buelcher	2.00
Henry Schaf	2.00
Patrick W. Shea	5.00
Geo. Schilling	5.00
John Coffey	1.00
James McDermott	1.00
John Conlin	2.00
Benjamin Riley	2.00
Wm. Rohm	1.00
Francis Wolf	5.00
Michael Molloy	1.00
William Ambos	1.00
Richard Carroll	5.00
Mrs. Keegan	2.00

Humboldt Street

Mr. Fitzpatrick	2.00
Michael Bannon	1.00
Mrs. Kelly	5.00
Jacob Bazell	1.00
P. J. O'Brien	5.00
Charles Mead	2.00
Mrs. Patrick Mead	5.00
Charles McAllister	2.00
Joseph Helmer	1.00
Andras Bach	1.00
Joseph Delaney	1.00
Mrs. Murphy	1.00
Michael Hanningan	1.00
John Crotty	3.00
Matthew Dugan	1.00
Roger McGill	2.00
Frank Brown	3.00

Humboldt Street

Adam Eich	3.00
John Clare	1.00
E. J. Davan	5.00
Wm. Gladding	2.00
Anonymous	1.00
Capt. Frederick Bauer	2.00
Ellen Quinn	1.00
Joseph Ester	1.00
Jane Ester	1.00
Charles Campbell	2.00
Frank Wearin	2.00
Augustus Frohne	1.00
Matthew Kennedy	2.00
Mrs. Whittaker	5.00
Mrs. Fay	5.00
Owen Loonan	5.00
Mrs. Blannan	2.00
James Gallagher	1.00
Thomas Duffy	5.00
Mrs. Quigley	2.00
Mrs. Hadley	2.00
Michael Ward	3.00
Mrs. M. Curran	2.00
George Higgins	1.00
John Flemming	2.00
Thomas Cady	5.00
Charles McDermott	1.00
A. McGill	3.00
Patrick Collins	3.00
Augustus Strumpfler	2.00
Mrs. Newton	3.00
Mamie Newton	1.00
Mary Kelly	1.00
James Conway	2.00
Michael Glavin	2.00
Helen Nillson	2.00
Geo. Rogers	1.00
Patrick Casey	5.00
Mary McQuinny	2.00

Humboldt Street

Mrs. Brophy	1.00
Peter Feisel	5.00
Mary Seidler	2.00
James Nolan	2.00
Joseph Voice	1.00
Mary Kiernan	5.00
Christopher Millbrawn	1.00
Rose Brady	1.00
Frank Kraemer	2.00
Vincent Spoth	5.00
Mrs. Kennard	1.00
Mrs. Curry	1.00
John Rossiter	2.00
Mrs. N. Becker	1.00
Mrs. Connolly	2.00
And. McGill	2.00
John Murphy	3.00

Hausman Street

Geo. Regan	$1.00
Maurice O'Leary	5.00
Edward Meehan	2.00
Maurice O'Connell	2.00
Patk. Foley	5.00
Frank Foley	1.00
Wm. Stratford	2.00
Daniel Toland	2.00
H. C. Schantz	2.00
M. Higgins	2.00

Herbert Street

John Sullivan	$1.00
J. J. Gavin	1.00
J German	1.00
John McHugh	2.00
John Hart	1.50
Miss Jane McCarthy	5.00
A. Clemens	1.00
In mem. H. McNeil	2.00
Mart. McCormack	2.00
John McCormack	2.00

Herbert Street

Miss A. Carolan	2.00
Ed Felsberg	1.00
Mrs. Hynes	5.00
James Doyle	5.00
Thomas McHugh	1.00
William Lace	5.00
Mrs. McGann	1.00
Joseph Miller	5.00
H. Miller	1.00
P. Catterson	1.00
S. Carpenter	1.00
Mrs. Whalen	1.00
H. Mellin	1.00
John Gately	1.00
Thos. Henry	1.00
Mrs. Mulhern	1.00
Mrs. B. Walsh	1.00
James D. Flynn	2.00
James H. Flynn	2.00
Louis Meyers	3.00
F. Shaefers	1.00
M. J. Campbell	5.00
Mrs. McDonough	2.00
P. J. Kenny	1.00
P. Spillane	2.00
Mrs. McMahon	2.00
M. Ormond	15.00
Cash	1.00
Mrs. Egan	2.00
John Hickey	5.00
H. O'Rourke	3.00
Thomas Carroll	1.00
P. Corby	2.00
John Brady	1.00
P. McKenna	1.00
John Conlon	1.00
John Elliot	1.00
Mrs. Neal	2.00
Charles Duhigg	1.00

Herbert Street

M. Dolan	2.00
P. Coyne	1.00
A. Dolan	2.00
Ed. Cassidy	25.00
Joseph Miller	2.00
Charles Byrne	2.00
B. Duhigg	5.00
Dr. B. Duhigg	5.00
Miss Margaret Kennedy	5.00
Miss Jane Gallagher	5.00
P. McDermott	1.00
D. Hanrahan	1.00
James Archibald	2.00
Mrs. M. Henry	5.00
M. McGuire	2.00
Mrs. McLinden	10.00
Charles Gugel	1.00
George Ford	2.00
John Glinnen's Sons	25.00
Charles Monahan	5.00
John Slattery	5.00
Ed McCusker	2.00
P. Garrahan	2.00
M. Quirk	2.00
Ch. O'Neil	2.00
John Gray	2.00

Broome Street

Thomas Murphy	$5.00
David G. Welch	1.00
John Taylor	1.00
James Grimshaw	2.00
Francis Thompson	2.00
Mary Malone	1.00
Bernard Brady	1.00
Albert Scheer	1.00
Peter Darmstedt	1.00
John McArdle	5.00
John Croal	2.50
Jacob Kohlmann	1.00

Broome Street

Edward Maher	2.00
Cornelius McMullin	2.00
John Kinceaid	2.00
Joseph Braun	2.00
William Healey	1.00
Terence McGuire	1.00
Christopher Walsh	1.00
John J. McCaffrey	1.00
D. Duhigg	2.00
Jas. Reddy	2.00

Powers Street

Mrs. Maguire	$5.00
Jacob Williams	5.00

Kingsland Avenue

Mrs. John Evans	$5.00
Mrs. Murphy	1.00
Mrs. Brenner	2.00
Patrick McCabe	2.00
Mrs. Reimling	1.00
Mary O'Neil	2.00
Mrs. Brown	2.00
James Colbert	5.00
Wm. McTighe	5.00
Timothy Foley	5.00
John Brennan	5.00
Wm. Farrell	3.00
Thomas Madden	2.00
Mrs. Drexler	1.00
John Connolly	1.00
Julian Guthrie	5.00
John Mulvaney	1.00
Thomas F. Gavin	2.00
Thomas Shanley	1.00
James Breen	1.00
Patrick Behn	2.00
John McDonald	5.00
William Matthews	2.00
Edward Davis	2.00
Mrs. Stanton	1.00

Kingsland Avenue

Catherine McCauley	3.00
Edward Plunkett	3.00
James Doyle	1.00
Mrs. McGinn	2.00
Michael Dooley	2.00
Timothy Gannon	3.00
John Quinn	1.00
Mrs. Sargeant	5.00
George Worden	10.00
Mrs. McCormack	5.00
Mrs. Bambush	2.00
Nicholas Walsh	1.00
Jacob Klueck	5.00
Jeremiah McCauley	5.00
Alfred Fovelle	1.00
Mrs. Whalen	1.00
James Cunningham	1.00
John Peterson	1.00
Patrick Lannon	2.00
John Brown	1.00
Mrs. Herberts	1.00
Mrs. Lane	5.00
Matt. Riley	2.00
Leopold Hoffman	1.00
Martin Mitchell	1.00
Sidney Manning	1.00
John Donohue	2.00
Linus Schuermann	1.00
John Woods	1.00
Michael Hynes	2.00
Theodore Eddy	1.00
Michael McBride	5.00
Edward Boyle	1.00
Catherine Schulein	5.00
Arthur Nugent	3.00
Patrick Holmes	5.00
George Neh	2.00
Mrs. Neh	1.00
Mrs. Purtell	1.00

Kingsland Avenue

Martin Trousdell	2.00
John Tully	2.00
Michael Trousdell	1.00
William Trousdell	1.00
Joseph Casey	1.00
Edward Wagner	1.00
Michael McNally	1.00
Mrs. White	1.00
Mrs. Linsky	1.00
Mrs. Fredericks	2.00
James Olwell	1.00
James King	1.00
Peter Crane	1.00
Dennis Griffin	1.00
Mrs. Murtha	1.00
Mrs. Leet	1.00
Mrs. Steppell	1.00
Mrs. McNally	2.00
Thomas Maloney	1.00
Mrs. Daley	1.00
Mary Shalby	1.00
Mrs. Santry	1.00
Joseph Skelly	1.00
Paul Kelly	1.00
Arthur Hadden	1.00
Mrs. Nelson	2.00
Mrs. Cameron	2.00
John Hynes	2.00
Thomas Meehan	2.00
Peter Kenna	1.00
Michael Ford	2.00
Bartholomew Mitchell	2.00
James Carlin	1.00
John W. Crilly	2.00
Mrs. Wolf	1.00

Metropolitan Avenue

Mrs. McKean	$1.00
John Lowrey	2.00

Nassau Avenue

Mrs. Reese	$10.00
P. F. Seymore	2.00
Paul Hausen	1.00
Thor Korsvig	2.00
E. J. Regan	2.00
Mrs. Blighe	1.00
John Shannon	1.00
John Becker	1.00
Arthur Breen	2.00
Mrs. Maguire	2.00
Malachi McGloin	5.00
T. Murray	1.00
Christ. Finnerty	1.00
James Donohue	2.00
M. Regney	2.00
James Ward	2.00
Thomas Collison	2.00
Charles Finnerty	1.00
M. Maher	1.00
John Shannon	1.00
T. Brosnan	2.00
James Shannon	1.00
Mrs. Shields	1.00
James Barker	1.00
William Davison	2.00
A. Lablotier	1.00
Ch. Hoenighausen	2.00
Mrs. Cath. Heffernan	5.00
Mrs. Casey	1.00
James Lynch	1.00
John Cummerford	3.00
Mrs. C. Vanderbilt	1.00
P. Wallace	2.00
Joseph Braun	2.00
Charles Connell	1.00
Mrs. E. Ebert	1.00
Miss Clarke	1.00
W. Schmelzle	1.00
F. Schmelzle	1.00

Nassau Avenue

Mrs. Zimmerman	1.00
Mrs. Otterbein	1.00
John McSheffrey	5.00
Arthur McSheffrey	1.00
Mrs. McCaffray	1.00
M. Muldoon	1.00
Ph. Feist	2.00
John Carnie	2.00
John Schail	1.00
John Kenna	2.00
James Tormey	2.00
John Englert	1.00
R. Kleisnitz	2.00
B. Ely	.50
D. Garnon	.50
T. Cummisky	3.00
B. Fagan	1.00
Mrs. Mahoney	1.00
Eug. Mahoney	5.00
Mrs. Fox	1.00
Miss Donohue	1.00
M. F. Dolan	5.00
P. McCormick	2.00
Thomas Conety	2.00
D. Collins	5.00
P. Lynch	1.00
Thomas Lynch	1.00
John Finnigan	1.00
J. Brady	.50
D. Kelly	3.00
W. Hannon	2.00
John Hannon	2.00
Mrs. Bruen	2.00
T. Fagan	1.00
James Shannon	2.00
J. J. Buckley	2.00
Thomas Murray	2.00
C. Gerhart	2.00
Denis Fogarty	5.00

Nassau Avenue

Mrs. Donnelly	1.00
R. Miller	3.00
Mrs. Albrecht	1.00
P. Kenna	1.00
John Finnigan	1.00
Thomas King	1.00
Kieran Rohan	2.00
James Caulfield	1.00
Sam O Neil	1.00
John Talty	2.00
P. Neary	3.00
G. Mahoney	5.00
Thomas Wehman	1.00
J. Wall	2.00
P. Gerrity	2.00
William Towle	1.00
Owen Malloy	2.00
Mrs. Costello	1.00
Mrs. Vaughin	3.00
Ed Duffy	1.00
Ed Gaff	3.00
P. Lynch	1.00
P. Hurley	2.00
P. Hannon	1.00
M. Byrne	2.00
James Logan, Jr.	2.00
John Kelly	2.00
M. Donohue	2.00
James Fagan	2.00
John McKenna	10.00
Miss Clarke	5.00

Bayard Street

Patrick Cassidy	2.00
Joseph Doyle	5.00
Mr. Kilpatick	5.00
George Fuchs	1.00
Patrick Rogers	1.00
John Laffy	5.00
Mrs. Hoffman	1.00

Maspeth Avenue

Pat'k Russell	$10.00
Thomas Lennon	5.00
John Burns	2.00
Michael Conden	2.00
Thos. Mulhearn	$2.00

North Henry Street

Henry J. Eisemann	$5.00
Charles J. Reilly	5.00
Charles Lang	5.00
John Gilroy	5.00
Christopher J. Doyle	5.00
Frank Farrell	5.00
Martin Rourke	10.00
David Glinnen	5.00
Arthur Donegan	2.00
Aron Lent	1.00
William Burt	1.00
William R. Sinnot	1.00
Christopher Bungart	2.00
James H. Gillen	5.00
Alex. McConeghy	5.00
James F. Burns	2.00
Daniel McCormick	1.00
Thomas Keating	1.00
Edward Degnan	2.00
Emily Eardly	1.00
William R. Brennan	5.00
Thomas Fitzpatrick	5.00
Henry Trageser	1.00
Patrick Trainor	1.00
Alexander Stephen	1.00
Charles Farrar	2.00
Margaret Courtney	1.00
Herbert Nixon	1.00
George F. Hall	1.00
Charles Farrar	1.00
Hiram Lawrence	1.00
James Doran	2.00
James Clark	3.00

North Henry Street

Patrick O'Neill	1.00
Catherine Whearty	1.00
Mary Farrell	1.00
John O'Toole	1.00
Charles Brown	3.00
Christopher Walters	2.00
John Cruice	2.00
Michael J. Nevins	5.00
Charles Stothard	2.00
John Bonneker	1.00
Catherine Fallon	1.00
George Helfenstein	1.00
John H. Pratt	2.00
Eliza Proctor	2.00
Angela Seiler	1.00
Joseph Kerrigan	1.00
Richard F. Adams	2.00
Michael Boyle	2.00
John Brosnan	1.00
Matthew Reynolds	1.00
John Hickey	1.00
Anthony Bursmann	1.00
Catherine Martin	1.00
"A Friend"	1.00
Bridget Reilly	2.00
Patrick Brady	2.00
Michael Brady	1.00
Mary Gross	1.00
John Corcoran	2.00
John Lang	1.00
Mrs. Stewart	2.00
William P. Murphy	1.00
Henry Miller	2.00
John Reilly	2.00
Martha Wilkinson	1.00
Winifred Hyland	1.00
William F. Snyder	1.00
Terence Sheridan	4.00
Donald Wendel	1.00

North Henry Street

Francis J. Connolly, Sr.	3.00
Francis J. Connolly, Jr.	3.00
Sarah Phelan	3.00
John E. Mahoney	5.00
Henry Steinhauer	5.00
John Smith	2.00
Louisa Smith	1.00
Thomas F. Dooley	3.00
Michael O'Gara	2.00
Luke Concannon	2.00
Edward Eagan	1.00
Eunice Gilloon	1.00
David H. Brother	2.00
James M. Tobin	5.00
Frederick Ahlborn	5.00
Mrs. Slowey	5.00

Engert Avenue

Thomas Kelly	$1.00
John McCabe	2.00
Thomas McDonald	1.00
Charles Haupt	1.00
Patrick Comer	1.00
William Plant	2.00
Geo. Herrmann	1.00
John McHugh	1.00
Henry Prummell	2.00
Timothy F. O'Grady	1.00
A Friend	5.00
Joseph E. Gough	1.00
Richard Reynolds	1.00
Edward Smith	3.00
Edward P. Parker	5.00
George F. Golden	5.00
Martin Gavin	5.00
Patrick Caufield	2.00
Honora Ward	1.00
Harriet Bogart	1.00
Charles Cobb	2.00
Matthew McAvoy	1.00

Engert Avenue

Charles Ryan	1.00
Bridget Connor	1.00
Robert Close	2.00
George Sweeting	1.00
Thomas McCormack	3.00
Mrs. Lewis	1.00
R. Taylor	2.00
J. McGinley	2.00
M. Burke	1.00

Union Avenue

John Donovan	$15.00
Martin Kelly	1.00
Mary Lamb	1.00
John Keenan	1.00
William Farmer	2.00
Margaret Farmer	2.00

Meeker Avenue

Cornelius Harty	$1.00
Mrs. Lynch	2.00
Mrs. Manfender	2.00
Malachi Glynn	1.00
James Mackin	2.00
John Churchill	1.00
James McCullough	2.00
Daniel Catterson	1.00
Thomas Golden	1.00
Martin Glynn	5.00
Thomas Glynn	1.00
Michael Kelly	2.00
Mrs. Bruen	1.00
Mrs. Conroy	1.00
John Rogan	5.00
John Sullivan	5.00
James Canty	2.00
James Dowd	1.00
Patrick Kelly	2.00
James Kelly	1.00
Edw. Cusack	1.00
John Connors	1.00

Meeker Avenue

John McAvoy	1.00
James O'Neil	1.00
Wm. Drohan	2.00
Mrs. Smith	2.00
John Neylan	1.00
John McDonell	1.00
Martin O'Donohue	1.00
Thomas McMahon	1.00
Anonymous	10.00
Michael Smith	1.00
William McErlane	1.00
Margaret Hunt	2.00
John Joyce	1.00
John O'Neil	5.00
Patrick O'Hare	2.00
William White	2.00
Wm. Corbett	5.00
Richard Downey	1.00
Ed. Nixon	1.00
John Rohr	2.00
Mrs. Britton	1.00
John F. Nolan	1.00
Mrs. Griffith	1.00
Patrick Fitzgerald	1.00
John Hannon	1.00
Matthew Cain	1.00
John Lowrey	1.00
Margaret Becker	2.00
Philip Freeworth	1.00
Thomas Becker	1.00
Mrs. Finnegan	2.00
J. J. Byrne	10.00
Mrs. Toner	10.00
Mrs. Blesser	5.00
Owen Foley	5.00
Patrick Condon	5.00
Mrs. Moran	1.00
B. Schieber	1.00
J. O'Shea	1.00

Meeker Avenue

John Cowley	2.00
John Gerrity	5.00
D. Sullivan	2.00
M. Connors	1.00
R. Seward	3.00
Joseph Drennan	1.00
Joseph Spatz	2.00
D. Donovan	5.00
J. Donovan	2.00
H. Phillips	1.00
Mrs. Capelli	1.00
William McIntyre	2.00
John Farrington	1.00
M. Phillips	1.00
John Buckley	2.00
Mrs. Cute	2.00
Laura Lang	1.00
Mrs. Discan	2.00
John Hannon	2.00
Mart. Carroll	1.00
L. McTighe	3.00
M. Kennedy	2.00
Herman Krott	1.00
Allan McDonald	2.00
P. Martin	1.00
Mrs. Flynn	1.00
M. Haevican	1.00
John Grimes	5.00
Mrs. Kelly	1.00
M. Walsh	1.00
P. Fleming	1.00
E. J. McAdams	3.00
John Grennan	1.00
Thomas Smith	1.00
P. Finnegan	1.00
John Powers	5.00
Mrs. Fitzpatrick	5.00
M. Quigley	5.00
Mrs. Staeger	1.00

Meeker Avenue

Miss M. Fitzpatrick	1.00
Mrs. Adams	2.00
F. Shields	1.00
Ed. McDonald	2.00
M. Connell	2.00
P. Gorman	10.00
William Gorman	5.00
R. Gorman	1.00
Mrs. McCormick	2.00
Chris Gorman	2.00
Joseph Brady	1.00
Mrs. Rakers	1.00

Lombardy Street

John Larkin	$2.00
John Hynes	5.00
Michael Hynes	1.00
John Hynes, Jr.	1.00
Thomas Solan	1.00
Andrew Kessler	1.00
Robert Handcock	5.00
Phil Gafney	1.00
John Campbell	3.00
Elizabeth Murphy	1.00
Michael Kelly	2.00
John Carr	2.00

Russell Street

James Kilroy	$5.00
J. McArdle	2.00
William McDonald	1.00
John Hickey	2.00
Mrs. O'Donnell	1.00
George Green	2.00
Charles Rassiga	2.00
A. Rulffs	1.00
Mrs. Smith	1.00
L. Geis	2.00
M. Donlon	2.00
M. McAlinden	5.00
Patrick Cunningham	2.00

Russell Street

Daniel O'Connell	1.00
Mrs. Daly	5.00
C. Nelson	4.00
F. Kiesler	1.00
P. O'Rourke	2.00
H. F. Roll	1.00
Peter Maley	1.00
J. Winkelman	.50
H. Braun	1.00
Joseph Clarke	3.00
F. Conradi	1.00
John O'Hare	5.00
Joseph Smith	3.00
Mrs. Rooney	5.00
John McMullen	1.00
John Nicholson	1.00
Mrs. Hughes	1.00
James O'Neil	2.00
P. J. Dempsey	2.00
Fred. Farrelly	1.00
M. Murphy	1.00
John Healy	1.50
James Kearney	2.00
B. Gallagher	2.00
C. Ward	1.00
M. J. Gillick	1.00
James McGinley	1.00
Cyriac deBrul	5.00
P. Fogarty	3.00
William Rodgers	5.00
James Rooney	5.00
P. McTiernan	10.00
F. Gilfillan	2.00
W. J. Shaw	5.00
M. Stanley	1.00
Mrs. Sheridan	1.00
T. Nesbit	1.00
John Kelly	1.00
R. Fickett	1.00

Russell Street

Miss McCaffray	2.00
Charles Ronan	5.00
John Shutta	5.00
L. Smith	2.00
Owen Gordon	2.00
John Delehanty	2.00
W. Allan	1.00
B. Langan	10.00
James Higgins	2.00
H. Daly	1.00
M. O'Leary	3.00
D. Ryan	1.00
J. S. Cassidy	2.00
James McNeelis	2.00
George Carroll	1.00
Rob Melvin	1.00

Lorimer Street

R. Caulfield	$10.00
M. Glennon	1.00
Mrs. Tuhl	1.00
Wm. Murphy	2.00
Dom. Blighe	1.00
J. E. Dooly	1.00
Patrick Catterson	3.00
M. Beck	.50
F. P. O'Neil	5.00
Bernard Hand	5.00
Owen Silk	1.00
James Flannigan	2.00
Mary Cullen	2.00
John Cullen	1.00
John Mullaney	2.00
John McDonald	1.00
William Keegan	1.00
James Mullaney	1.00
Thomas Clougher	1.00
John Fitzsimmons	1.00
Thomas McCormick	1.00
Mary Norton	1.00

Lorimer Street

Patrick Kane	5.00
Patrick Daley	1.00
Charles Rohme	1.00
James Winchester	1.00
John O'Neil	1.00
Patrick Keavney	2.00
Joseph Marsh	2.00
Mrs. J. Sleight	1.00

Skillman Avenue

Thomas Ward	$2.00
Patrick Hynes	2.00
J. Finnegan	5.00
Mrs. Velsor	1.00
Thomas Derrick	5.00
Daniel Shea	1.00
Mrs. Weidner	1.00
Jacob Sedelmeyer	2.00
Michael Sullivan	5.00
Thos. Parks	5.00
Mrs. Sweeney	5.00
Hubert Neil	1.00
J. Briggs	2.00
Jas. A. Calhoun	1.00
Mrs. Barthold	1.00
Michael McKenna	1.00
Mrs. Nolan	1.00
Michael Leonard	5.00
Miss McElroy	1.00
Elizabeth Connoughton	1.00
Jas. Coleman	5.00
William Hughes	1.00
John Colwell	2.00
Miss Mohan	$5.00

Driggs Avenue

John O'Rourk	$1.00
Thomas Brennan	1.00
Michael O'Brien	2.00
William Heck	2.00
Peter Mullin	1.00

Driggs Avenue

Emil Kornrumpf	2.00
Wm. Murphy	3.00
Ed. Farnon	2.00
James Sheridan	2.00
Mrs. Mary Gafney	1.00
Annie Beisel	1.00
John O'Reilly	1.00
Mrs. Keane	1.00
John Foley	1.00
Mrs. Kane	1.00
John Mooney	5.00
Mr. Holohan	1.00
James Conway	1.00
Patrick Gallagher	1.00
Henry Hoch	2.00
Patrick Donnelly	1.00
John Cunningham	2.00
James Fitzgerald	1.00
James Kelly	2.00
Michael Watson	2.00
Timothy Touhey	1.00
Mrs. Schuler	1.00
Michael Clancy	2.00
Frank McElearney	1.00
Thomas Daly	1.00
Bryan Gilroy	10.00
Michael Quinn	1.00
Patrick Purtell	1.00
Michael Crotty	1.00
Patrick Flynn	1.00
Mrs. Witzel	1.00
E. J. Clifford	2.00
Daniel McTammeny	1.00
Michael Conroy	1.00
Frank Schevlevin	1.00
Michael Collins	1.00
Patrick Gafney	2.00
Martinus Martens	1.00
Edward Garrity	1.00

Driggs Avenue

Mrs. Miller	1.00
Mrs. Merrigan	5.00
Michael Kelly	5.00
Thomas Shannon	1.00
Michael Tierney	1.00
John Kerwick	2.00
Wm. McCarthy	1.00
Charles O'Brien	1.00
Catherine Kissane	1.00
Mr. Donnelly	10.00
Mrs. McElroy	3.00
Mrs. Eberts	1.00
John Cahill	1.00
Michael McNamara	2.00
P. J. Boylan	1.00
Patrick Gilroy	5.00
Mrs. Elliot	1.00
Patrick Crane	1.00
John Tucker	2.00
Cornelius Tucker	1.00
J. M. Farrell	2.00
W. Armstrong	1.00
P. Crilly	3.00
Mrs. McVickar	1.00

Frost Street

Catherine Delay	$1.00
Mary Keegan	5.00
Peter Ward	2.00
William Coar	1.00
Michael Lahey	2.00
Thomas Kelley	2.00
Henry Young	1.00
Jane Brown	2.00
Thomas Garrity	1.00
Denis O'Leary	5.00
James Ryan	2.00
Owen Campbell	5.00
John Donnelly	5.00
Lawrence Gowen	2.00

Frost Street

Thomas Rogers	1.00
Mary Meskell	1.00
Michael Adams	2.00
John Hamill	1.00
James Keenan	1.00
John Schuler	1.00
John Joyce	1.00
Terence Murphy	2.00
Hannah Garathy	1.00
Charles Shade	2.00
Peter Fitzpatrick	2.00
Denis Kelleher	2.00
Martin Giff	2.00
Mary Mulcahey	1.00
Sarah Cain	10.00
Sarah McLaughlin	5.00
Eugene Montague	5.00
Mary Holt	2.00
Albert Rose	1.00
James Butler	1.00
Sarah Jones	5.00
John Reilly	5.00
Charles Schule	1.00
Eugene McCaffrey	2.00
Sarah Hayes	1.00
Catherine McGuire	2.00
John Kelley	2.00
John Coleman	1.00
Mary Nolan	5.00
Mrs. Drennan	1.00
Thomas Smith	1.00
James Campbell	3.00

Bedford Avenue

Cash	$10.00
John Boyan	2.00
Eliza Mellis	1.00
Al. Stoltz	1.00
Mrs. Grady	5.00
Thomas Grady	1.00

Bedford Avenue

John Free	3.00
James Gavin	2.00

Monitor Street

Edward Donovan	$5.00
William Riley	5.00
Ann Madden	2.00
Daniel J. Collins	5.00
Mary Byrne	1.00
Henry Herman	1.00
James Slattery	5.00
James Rossiter	1.00
Maria Britt	2.00
Miss Mack	1.00
Patrick Trousdell	3.00
Catherine Limmer	1.00
Daniel Reardon	2.00
Alfred Scheffler	2.00
James Bogan	1.00
Wm. A. Smith	2.00
William Tierney	1.00
John Donovan	2.00
Anthony McGourty	2.00
William Haley	1.00
James Dunn	2.00
Joseph Fletcher	2.00
John Fox	1.00
Ellen Grasson	1.00
Patrick Blanchfield	3.00
J. R. Engelskiger	1.00
John Hessler	1.00
William Parnell	2.00
William Mulligan	5.00
Thomas A. Clark	2.00
James J. Fanning	5.00
Edward Moeller	1.00
John F. Borre	2.00
John O'Neill	2.00
William Murphy	1.00
B. M. Jones	1.00

Monitor Street

George E. McCaffrey	2.00
Joseph Painting	5.00
James Dillon	5.00
Valentine Trageser	2.00
Edward Murray	2.00
John Nelson	2.00
Thomas Bennett	1.00
Margaret Walker	2.00
Mary Leonard	2.00
Henry Martin	5.00
James McNiff	5.00
John T. Brown	5.00
John Bostrom	3.00
Charles Quinn	3.00
John Conlin	5.00
Michael J. Casey	2.00
Thomas Dolan	5.00
Martin Clair	5.00
Patrick J. Sullivan	3.00
William Hampton	1.00
Jos. Swinsky	2.00
Emma De Ryck	2.00
Ella A. McConnin	2.00
Mrs. Newport	1.00

Sutton Street

Peter Keilback	$1.00
M. Treacy	3.00
George W. Treacy	2.00
M. Marrenan	1.00
John Meanick	3.00
K. O'Brien	5.00
John Waldron	1.00
John Wallace	2.00
Frank Costello	5.00
Thomas Costello	2.00
August Costello	2.00
John Weber	1.00
Mrs. Roach	.50
Mrs. Kaufman	1.00

Sutton Street

M. McAuley	1.00
John O'Hara	1.00
James Creeden	5.00
Patrick Creeden	1.00
P. Costello	1.00
N. Drennan	1.00
T. Donohue	2.00
John Cox	1.00
A. Guinan	1.00
Thomas Flemming	1.00
O. Moran	1.00
J. Estelle	1.00
M. Hurley	5.00
M. Hurley, Jr.	2.00
Wm. Ryan	2.00
F. Gaffney	1.00
P. Clarke	1.00
Charles Ward	2.00
E. J. McArdle	.50
Thomas Waldron	1.00
John Lee	2.00
Mrs. Gill	1.00
Mrs. Fields	1.00
Harry Connolly	1.00
James Dollard	5.00
Thos. Davis	5.00

Richardson Street

Mrs. Doyle	$2.00
Joseph Stoecker	2.00
Mary Taggett	5.00
John Robertson	1.00
Mrs Curry	1.00
Mrs. M. Donovan	5.00
John Burnsides	5.00
Mrs. Fitsimmons	2.00
Joseph Saunders	2.00
Geo. Koerner	2.00
Stephen Goodyear	1.00
Mary J. Johnson	2.00

Richardson Street

Bridget Wolf	1.00
William Keenan	1.00
Lawrence Coughlin	1.00
Charles Hess	1.00
John Clougher	1.00
Patrick Quinn	1.00
Ed. Cusick	1.00
Mrs. Collins	1.00
Peter Green	$2.00

Withers Street

Mrs. McQuillan	$2.00
James McQuillan	1.00
Ann Clark	3.00
Cath. Lynch	1.00
Catherine Fitzpatrick	5.00
Mrs. Elizabeth Kelleher	5.00
James Kelleher	3.00
Margaret Fitzpatrick	2.00
John Brown	2.00
Mrs. Fitzpatrick	1.00
Geo. DeWalters	1.00
Wm. Breslin	5.00
Wm. Wilmot	5.00
Richard Godsil	5.00
Mr. McEneaney	2.00
Mrs. Hart	1.00
Mrs. Longein	1.00
James McGuire	1.00
John Merrick	1.00
Margaret Carr	1.00
Mrs. Doerfler	1.00
Mrs. Reilly	10.00
Owen Reilly	1.00
John Golden	5.00
Lawrence Hoar	2.00
John Ackerman	2.00
Ann Shea	1.00
Jas. Hanifin	1.00
Wm. Skehan	5.00

Withers Street

Mary Kenny	1.00
Julia Cunningham	2.00
Jas. Miller	2.00
Thomas F. Elliott	1.00
Mary Smith	1.00
G. Sherry	1.00
Geo. Keenan	3.00
Thos. Keenan	3.00
Phil Taggart	1.00
Michael Kerrigan	2.00
Michl. Cooney	2.00
Jas. F. Kelly	2.00
Geo. Leonard	2.00
James Battersby	2.00
John Connolly	3.00
Geo. McDonough	2.00
Arthur Donegan	1.00
Thos. Donegan	1.00
Frances Langan	2.00
James Curran	2.00
Owen Keenan	15.00
Mary Keenan	10.00
John Wedlock	2.00
Frank Weisbecker	5.00
And. Marquart	5.00
Augustus Jacobi	2.00
Grace McGeary	1.00
Isabella Curran	2.00
Mrs. Fletcher	3.00

Graham Avenue

William Nowlin	$2.00
Henry Robinson	3.00
Charles Albrecht	15.00
John Howard	1.00
Barbara & Carrie Bohne	1.50
Jacob Gerner	1.00
Bridget Connell	1.00
Cath. & Lillian Reilly	2.00
Edward White	1.00

Graham Avenue

Barbara Kotz	2.00
Frederick Bienfeld	1.00
Ann Will	1.00
Wm. J. Chaffers	2.00
Michael Quinn	5.00
Peter Dolan	1.00
Michael Connolly	2.00
Richard Travis	2.00
Frank Lorenz	1.00
Patrick Ward	1.00
Michael Foley	2.00
John L. Moore	2.00
M. Archibald	2.00
Thomas Scott	1.00
John O'Connor	5.00
Arthur Collins	1.00
Charles Wolf	2.00
Joseph McAuley	2.00
Mrs. Dunn	1.00
Mrs. Collier	1.00
Mart. Collier	1.00
Ed Carroll	17.00
Mrs. Hilkenback	5.00
Joseph Tammany	2.00
Charles Dowd	15.00
Peter Monahan	2.00
Miss Nunan	5.00
William Ward	2.00
Charles O'Neil	.50
Louis Phillipps	1.00
John Gorman	2.00
Joseph McAlister	8.00
John Lee	5.00
John Rockenbrod	3.00
M. Bellinger	3.00
T. J. Maguire	2.00
M. Carolan	1.00
John Gorman	2.00
John Mahoney	8.00

Graham Avenue

John Jacobs	1.00
M. Mullen	1.00
John Kuhl	5.00

Guernsey Street

Mrs. E. McConaghy	$2.00
Jos. Callahan	2.00
John Daniels	4.00
William Daniels	5.00

Jewell Street

Charles Brustman	$2.00
Thomas Delaney	1.00
James Donohue	1.00
Patrick Donohue	3.00

Greenpoint Avenue

J. Manley	$5.00
D. Coan	1.00
Owen Duffy	1.00
Mrs. M. Tuohy	1.00

Manhattan Avenue

Mary Hoar	$5.00
Margaret Twohil	5.00
Rosanna Coffey	1.00
Bridget Donoghue	1.00
Patrick Courtney	1.00
Richard Blake	1.00
Louisa Heinstaedt	1.00
Ann Barry	1.00
August Siegert	2.00
Bridget McAvoy	1.00
Philip Blake	1.00
Thomas McCann	2.00
Edward Monney	1.00
Edward J. Flannagan	5.00
William Donovan	5.00
Joseph J. Lovell	5.00
Mrs. O'Neil	2.00
F. Pendleton	1.00
M. Hughes	2.00
W. H. Burrows	2.25

Manhattan Avenue

Thomas Sullivan	1.00
Mrs. Monks	2.00
Mrs. Connolly	5.00
Mrs. Reynolds	1.00
Daniel Enright	2.00
P. Hanaghan	2.00
Mrs. Fallon	1.00
John Gaffney	1.00
Mrs. Croaley	.50
M. Kelly	5.00
P. J. O'Neil	2.00
P. Maloney	1.00
N. Birmingham	5.00
F. Birmingham	2.00
James Flynn	5.00
James Cassidy	2.00

Leonard Street

Patrick F. Carroll	$5.00
Ann Brady	2.00
D. & F. Brady	5.00
Ann Martin	2.00
John Brady	1.00
Michael McGeary	2.00
Alice Muldoon	2.00
Bridget Crawford	1.00
Edward Clark	1.00
Michael Collins	1.00
Jane Weeks	1.00
Thomas Kelley	5.00
Ed. Kennedy	1.00
Mrs. Olmstead	5.00
John Daly	1.00
R. Meadows	2.00
John McMahon	2.00
Charles McDonald	1.00
John Oesterman	2.00
J. J. McCullough	2.00
Charles Rogers	1.00
James Foley	2.00

Eckford Street

James Butler	$5.00
P. Clappan	1.00
Miss Maloney	2.00
Arch. McVicar	5.00
D. McDowell	1.00
F. Ackerman	1.00
F. D. Maguire	2.00
Mrs. Caffrey	5.00
Charles McNeil	2.00
M. McGrath	2.00
Clem. Schmitz	5.00
John Durack	1.00
C. McDevitt	1.00
M. J. Carney	1.00
George Bolger	2.00
Mrs. B. Nearney	2.00
H. Mehlig	2.00
D. O'Hara	1.00
Th. Newell	.50
Charles Smith	1.00
Mrs. Leo	1.00
M. White	1.00
John McCullom	1.00
J. J. Connolly	1.00
Elizabeth McGee	1.00

Jackson Street

Thomas Havican	$1.00
William Breslin	2.00
John Lally	2.00
Mrs. Lockard	2.00
Charles E. Skehan	10.00
Mrs. Grimes	2.00
John Schaefer	1.00
William Thornton	5.00
Patrick Meegan	3.00
Mrs. Leahy	2.00
F. Jensens	1.00
Mrs. De Hert	2.00
John McDermott	1.00

Jackson Street

James Nicholson	1.00
Mrs. Doyle	5.00
D. Murphy	2.00
Mrs. Herbert	1.00
P. Cassidy	3.00
L. Young	2.00
Mrs. Holz	2.00
J. W. Williams	1.00
Rosanna Doyle	3.00
Ann Meyer	1.00
Joseph Vorbach	1.00
Bridget Daley	2.00
Patrick Shea	2.00
Ann Costello	2.00
Peter Clark	5.00
Robert Swift	1.00
Mary Abel	1.00
Jeremiah Kieley	2.00
Cornelius Foley	1.00
John Owen	2.00
Ernest Ebert	4.00
Francis Jankowiak	2.00
James Mulvaney	1.00
Rose Mary Morrissey	$5.00

Oakland Street

James Mullaney	$1.00
M. Nolan	1.00
Ed. Ulrick	1.00
Mrs. Mandrey	5.00
Joseph B. Mahoney	1.00
John McEntee	1.00
John Riley	2.00
Thomas Shaw	1.00
Mrs. Haslipp	2.00
Mrs. McKenna	1.00
Thomas Kilmartin	1.00
P. F. Kohlman	5.00
John Looney	2.00
H. Rowe	2.00

Oakland Street

M. G. Quinlan	10.00
P. H. Craddock	5.00
H. Bradisich	2.00
G. Smith	2.00
F. Gilloon	1.00
Mrs. Joyce	2.00
James Flynn	3.00
John McKay	2.00
A. Hultz	1.00

Newell Street

Catherine McEroe	$1.00
James Hughes	3.00
Mrs. Toole	5.00
Thomas Demskie	1.00
Mrs. Kelly	1.00
Ph. Kelly	2.00
Robert Anderson	.50
Cash	.50
James Kane	1.00
John J. McHenry	1.00
P. Divine	3.00
Mrs. Wright	5.00
Benjamin Wright	1.00
P. Callanan	2.00
J. J. Duane	2.00
H. Derricks	1.00
James Corbett	1.00
Mrs. Meegan	5.00
Bart. Heany	1.00
M. McGowan	1.00
Kenneth Clancy	1.00
Ellen Fitzgerald	1.00
M. Kjoback	1.00
Mrs. Biggett	2.00
Mrs. Kiernan	5.00
Thomas Kiernan	2.00

Diamond Street

M. Coyne	$1.00
D. Long	1.00

Diamond Street

J. Blaney	3.00
Mrs. O'Keeffe	2.00
A. Wolz	1.00
J. Carey	2.00
Joseph Boylan	1.00
Thomas Fisher	2.00
Mrs. M. English	2.00
Mrs. Kelly	2.00
D. Wheeler	1.00
F. Warburton	1.00
Miss Crowley	2.00
Mrs. O'Neill	3.00
R. Newell	3.00
Mrs. Manley	1.00
R. Arndt	1.00
E. Kelly	1.00
William Flaherty	1.00
John Condon	2.00
Mrs. A. Gallagher	3.00
L. Eisner	2.00
Thomas Logan	2.00
J. McKillop	2.00
James O'Neil	1.00
D. Lyons	1.00
John Maloney	1.00
John Melaniff	2.00
James Mace	2.00
Miss E. Mace	2.00
P. Kenny	2.00
Charles Conklin	1.00
P. Harding	3.00
John Ward	2.00
Mrs. McGoldrick	3.00
George Zolver	3.00
William Mullet	1.00
M. Fallon	5.00

Norman Avenue

Thomas Treacy	$2.00

Norman Avenue

J. McCabe	3.00
J. C. Vetter	4.00
Joseph O'Brien	1.00

Conselyea Street

Martin Leach	$2.00
A. Fitzgibbons	1.00
Joseph M. Collins	3.00
William Bardlesmas	1.00
P. Gorman	1.00
Mrs. E. Yard	5.00
Ed Zettsman	.50

Old Bushwick Road

Patrick Devine	$2.00
Thomas J. Ryan	1.00
Thomas Callahan	1.00

Morgan Avenue

Patk. Neuman	$10.00
John Mullins	1.00
Mrs. Westlake	2.00
David Quinlan	10.00
Richard Cloke	5.00

Varick Street

R. Dobbins	$2.00

Newton Street

Valentine Hill	$1.00
William Watson	2.00
James Green	5.00
John Whalen	1.00

Division Place

Geo. Brady	$1.00

Banzett Street

John Shea	$5.00
James O'Connor	1.00
Wm. Dillon	5.00
Chas. Uhlinger	2.00

Grand Total, $4,476.00

THE RIGHT REVEREND JOHN LOUGHLIN LYCEUM.

When, in 1888, Father McGolrick came to shepherd St. Cecilia's flock, the little shed, that had, in 1870, served as part of the first Church, was still in existence and acting as a Club House for "The Young Men's Literary Society of St. Cecilia's."

The present Supreme Court Judge of King's County, New York, Charles J. Dodd, was one of the members of the Club and even then, at the young age of fifteen years, his oratory made such favorable impression upon his fellows that the Club christened him "Chauncey Depew."

The name of the society sounded auspicious but when I questioned the Pastor, his eyes twinkled and a smile came o'er his face, the smile that has doubtless checked many a controversy, smoothed out many a difficulty for him during the forty-two years he has been in charge of the parish. It reminded me of what his classmate had written of the Manhattan boy's thorough enjoyment of a good joke when the dignified Monsignor replied:

"Well, they had very few books and they were seldom opened. The young men of that literary society were very busy, you know, in the use and care of their boxing-gloves."

The truth is, the young Pastor was greatly pleased with the Literary part of the Society and he was really not displeased with the boxing gloves. He recognized that true education is triune—the development of body, mind and soul. Here was at least some slight show of self-development along the mental, a little more along the physical, and he knew the Church to which these young men belonged had for its mission the giving from altar, pulpit and confessional certain rich growth along the spiritual.

Of the twelve or fourteen young men present at that first meeting, ten of them volunteered to act as ushers in the Church. One young man, John Kelly, was too modest to volunteer for an office which would necessitate his walking up and down the aisles of a church filled with worshippers. But his comrades forced him into it. And once in the work, he remained a faithful usher for more than thirty years. When his name was mentioned, in the recall of early days, the present Monsignor said in an unmistakably feeling tone: "May he rest in peace."

A resolution was born in Father McGolrick's heart when first he entered that crude club room that these earnest, honest young men should receive from him every possible encouragement, looking to the growth and cultivation of their reading and the refining of their sport, and the young men coming after them in the parish would have a fitting place in which to meet.

Out of this resolution, came the Lyceum. As soon as the present St. Cecilia edifice was completed, the old frame church, which had been moved from its original site, was greatly enlarged and placed upon a new and sure foundation. The corner-stone that had been blessed by Bishop Loughlin in 1871, was reversed now to serve as the corner-stone of the Right Reverend John Loughlin Memorial Lyceum, popularly called the Loughlin Lyceum.

This commodious building was completed in the year 1903 and is a grand adjunct of the school and church. In it may be found splendid aids to physical development—a well-equipped gymnasium, bowling alleys, billiard tables and swimming pool accessible during the summer vacation months as well as throughout the school year. For the advancement of the mind there are reading rooms and a large auditorium with a seating capacity of six hundred and with a roomy and well-furnished stage.

The writer has faced two overflowing audiences in this splendid parochial hall and has found an appreciative, dignified, intelligent response not surpassed by any audience in any section of the country where she has been privileged to lecture. Such response has doubtless grown out of the rich opportunities and excellent training granted St. Cecilia's parishioners through their Lyceum.

The *Brooklyn Daily Times* describing this building says:
"This structure is a modern institution, elegantly fitted up with a complete equipment for dramatic, social, educational and physical efforts. Its yearly calendar is a complete circuit of gala and joyous gatherings where priest and people meet and the young and old come together for social enjoyment."

Loughlin Lyceum is also the place where much practical aid is given to the many charitable projects within the parish and it lends itself as freely to help needy and suffering humanity the wide world over.

The many and varied Societies of the parish hold their meetings here. Here, too, is served each May the yearly after-Communion breakfast of the loyal Alumnae of St. Cecilia's School.

It speaks well for the priests and the congregation that societies formed in the parish do not dwindle in numbers or in vigor. All Societies which first met in the Lyceum at its opening, twenty-seven years ago, are still in existence and, as the Pastor puts it "going strong."

To the school children what an advantage such building gives. Out of such halls as this have sprung the O'Connors, the Cochranes, and the Augustin Dalys of our land. Even if fame like to theirs is never sought, conversation, itself a charming art, is here developed. Here the worth and work of words is learned for in debate the value of their choice and the necessity of their expressive delivery is made manifest. And how admirably all this fits in with preparation for the legal profession or the priesthood. Whether continued to such exalted heights or not, it greatly helps to round out the persuasive power of the individual in any walk of life.

The Lyceum with its excellent equipment for physical development, its reading rooms and auditorium for greater mental attainment is more than ever a necessity in this day when the automobile induces bodily inactivity and wheels so many away from all mental effort, all mental enjoyment; and when Movie and Talkie supply for young and old alike a predigested brain food that stunts, where it does not actually poison, brain cells.

THE McGOLRICK RECREATION FIELD.

If in nature, the lambs skip and the rivers sing why shouldn't man have his hours of active, joyous forgetfulness of care, health-giving hours of cessation from business anxieties. From the very beginning, Father McGolrick wanted a playground for his people; wanted a playground that the school children might use every day, and the grown-ups might occasionally enjoy. All beginnings are difficult. But a brave heart is not hedged by difficulty. The idea of providing a place where his parishioners might indulge in wholesome, well-directed outdoor sport would not down in Father McGolrick's heart. At first a few vacant lots in the Bushwick section became a kind of squatters' field of fun for the young folks. Here the boys of St. Cecilia's parish played baseball and practised running and jumping. Here a number of important parish events took place. From *The Citizen* of June 22, 1907 we cull the following interesting article:

COLER GUEST OF HONOR AT MILITARY CARNIVAL.

Greeted With Cheers at the Loughlin Oval.

FATHER McGOLRICK PRAISED.

Exhibition of Athletics Given Under Electric Lights—Drill by
Loughlin Battalion.

Borough President Coler was the guest of honor last night
at the military carnival held in the Loughlin Oval, at Kingsland Avenue and Jackson Street, for the benefit of the new
parochial school of St. Cecilia's parish. He was accorded an
enthusiastic ovation when he made his appearance in the
extensive grounds where the festival is being held. Mr. Coler
was escorted into the oval by the Rev. Edward J. McGolrick,
the pastor of the church, and a committee consisting of James
Fitzpatrick, the chairman of the Ways and Means Committee;
Joseph Reydel, August Frohne and James Lawrence. Acting
as a guard of honor was the Loughlin' Drum and Fife Corps.
This organization and the committee met the Borough President in another church on Conselyea Street, where he had
promised to be. Mr. Coler had his own auto. When he
walked into the oval a great cheer went up from the multitude
gathered near the front entrance. Everything was in full swing
at the time. The merry-go-rounds were being operated to their
fullest capacity, while all the booths were being liberally
patronized. The night was known as Hibernian night, and it
brought to the oval almost a full attendance of the members
of Divisions 9 and 23. Nearly all of these brought along their
families. Father McGolrick is the chaplain of No. 9, and this
organization had its full strength on hand. The members
were not in uniform.

After Mr. Coler had been shown around the grounds he
was escorted to the platform, where he addressed a large

gathering and paid a high compliment to Father McGolrick for his efficient work in the parish and for his indefatigable efforts in trying to get the new school building. Mr. Coler went on to say that with the active co-operation of his parishioners Father McGolrick was bound to succeed.

Mr. Coler was heartily applauded at the close of his remarks. Meanwhile many crack athletes had arrived at the grounds and they gave some fine exhibitions of their athletic prowess. There was Con Walsh, the Irish champion weight-thrower; John J. Flanagan, the champion hammer-thrower; Lawson Robertson, the champion sprinter; James Archer, of New York; P. L. Waters, the junior American champion; Martin Sheridan, the world's champion all-around athlete; J. J. Joyce, the three-mile champion; James H. Teevan, the champion of Canada; Frank W. Riley, junior American champion; Charles Conlon, champion sprinter of Brooklyn, and Martin Cowan and Martin Sheridan, who gave an exhibition of throwing the javelin. All the exhibitions were given under powerful electric lights.

There was a parade of 200 girls dressed in white and wearing the national colors. Louis Hannweber had trained and rehearsed them, and the little paraders made such a fine appearance that even the Borough President was obliged to praise them by hand-clapping. The Loughlin battalion gave an exhibition drill under the direction of their commander, Major John L. Moore. When they wound up it was in the form of three letters, "A. O. H.," meaning "Ancient Order of Hibernians." Great applause greeted them.

It was not long, however, until the Loughlin oval was purchased by the City for a Hospital site.

In that dark hour, it looked to the Pastor and his boys as if there never would be another chance for a baseball diamond or a track. Real estate prices had been mounting—vacant lots

ST. CECILIA ATHLETES

in the vicinity of St. Cecilia's Church could not be had for a song, and a Recreation Field worth the name would require a good many lots. Right at this point a woman enters in. I like to tell the story for, ever since man's expulsion from Paradise, all things evil have been blamed on woman. It's a positive treat to find some really good enterprise attributed to the work of a woman's tongue.

One of St. Cecilia's girls, a Miss Ella Finnigan, was working in the William E. Harmon Real Estate Office at 261 Broadway. Fifteen or twenty other young ladies from various Catholic parishes in Greater New York were likewise engaged in office work there. At noon time they frequently discussed the relative merits of their churches and Pastors. One day Miss Finnegan's voice rose above the others loyally extolling her own Pastor as the first best. From the adjoining room the President of the Company caught the trend of the speaker's enthusiastic praise. He was not a Catholic, though he had been educated by the Jesuits in Texas, and revered the practices of the Faith. He concluded, as he listened to Miss Finnigan, that the priest who had done so much for his people and had won from them such unqualified loyalty must be a good man to meet. He sought such meeting. Out of it grew a friendship which was only terminated when death took Mr. Harmon.

And what's the story? Well, a little later when Mr. Harmon heard of the loss of the playground, he set to work to second the Pastor's efforts. He secured an entire square of city lots in close proximity to the Church at the low price of twenty-one thousand dollars. He himself donated three thousand and was instrumental in obtaining another three thousand donation. The leveling of the field, building a high stone wall around it and erecting a grand stand added twenty-five thousand dollars to the cost. But what return has come from such expenditure!

The Pastor Blessing the McGolrick Recreation Field

If it be that the crowded marts of the great city hatch vice, then is it equally true that the open space and generous grounds of the Recreation Field inspire virtue. At least it is a known fact that outdoor exercise does not invite sin. The body is God's handiwork and its rights are never more regarded than when fresh air fills the lungs and happy competitive sport sends the blood coursing through the veins with the hope of victory wholesomely thrilling the nerves. In the McGolrick Recreation Field both the healthful and delightful are subserved, for here effort, laughter and enthusiasm join in free camaraderie. It has brought much attention to the athletic prowess of St. Cecilia's boys. For five years they swept everything in the Inter-Parochial School League conducted by the Christian Brothers, in Greater New York. In all track work they carried off the laurels.

The Field is not confined to parochial use only. It serves as a neighborhood playground during vacation months, a community playground under Catholic auspices, bestowing on St. Cecilia's parish a truly distinguishing mark along a very necessary and charitable line.

We hope for the McGolrick Recreation Field such longevity as a playground in the very heart of busy London enjoys —a playground which was set aside for the youngsters in the tenth century and has not yet been diverted from its original purpose.

Monsignor McGolrick Throwing Out the First Ball

A LETTER FROM WM. E. HARMON.

125 Willow Street,
Brooklyn, New York,
April 20/21.

Dear Monsignor:

I was delighted to get your note. It is a beautiful thing to realize the constancy of a friendship between busy men like you and me. I often think of you.

A message like the one I have just finished reading, warms my heart and makes me know that our mutual love is permanent.

It is true. I have had a nasty attack and one from which I am fortunate in making so good a recovery. Am sitting up about two hours a day but my lungs are wheezing and only working, I think, on one cylinder.

Remember, dear Monsignor, that your letters and kind thoughts do me lots of good.

Affectionately,

Wm. E. Harmon.

OUTSPOKEN DENIAL.

An article, appearing in the April 27th, 1908, issue of the *New York Evening Telegram* is in keeping with the honesty and fearlessness of the priest who has from his earliest boyhood believed in the recreative value of out-door sports.

BROOKLYN PRIEST SCORES HUGHES'
ANTI-RACING BILL.

Father McGolrick Says the Church and Not the State
Can Make Men Better.

Several clergymen in Brooklyn were much surprised and annoyed to-day to learn that the promoters of a gathering to uphold Governor Hughes' anti-racing campaign had used their names without authorization in sending out calls for a mass meeting. Among these was the Rev. Father Edward J. McGolrick, of St. Cecilia's Roman Catholic Church, who was said to be supporting the fight. Father McGolrick stated that, on the contrary, he was not in favor of the measure the Governor is pushing.

"I think it is entirely beyond the province of a Legislature to attempt such a thing. It belongs to the Church and the home to make men better. As Cardinal Gibbons says impossible restrictions tend to make men hypocrites. In this connection I noticed during the recent vote on the anti-racing bill at Albany that one Senator, who had been out all night and admitted having won $2,000 in a poker game, rejoiced that he had returned to the Senate Chamber in time to record his vote in favor of Governor Hughes' over-zealous endeavor to destroy a sport which flourishes in every other country but this—a sport known the world over as the 'sport of kings.'

"I want to state," continued Father McGolrick, "that I gave no authority to anybody to use my name in connection with any movement having for its object the abolition of racing. There are of course incidental evils in connection with racing, but are there not evils connected with every sport? Men can degrade the serious occupations of life. Betting is not an evil in itself. Life is a speculation; so is business. A man invests $1,000 in some enterprise with the expectation of making a profit. He may win, and he may lose. The spirit of gaming is as old as civilization. Men wager on all sorts of eventualities."

ST. CECILIA'S DAY NURSERY.

The Secretary of "St. Cecilia's Day Nursery Association" submits the following report concerning the formation of this most charitable society and of the establishment and upkeep of the Parish Day Nursery.

"On Tuesday, October 18, 1904, Father McGolrick addressed one hundred ladies, assembled in Loughlin Lyceum, on the great need of a Day Nursery in St. Cecilia's parish.

"The object of the Day Nursery would be to assist parents bereft of their helpmates to keep their homes intact by caring for their little ones while they were at work. It would also take the place of the St. Vincent de Paul Society.

"To the satisfaction of all present, it was decided to form an association which would assume the responsibility of such an undertaking, said association to be called *St. Cecilia's Day Nursery Association.*

"The members were to support the Nursery by their dues, social affairs and donations. An additional support would be all money collected for candles burned in the church during a period of three weeks in every month.

"In return, the members were to benefit in a spiritual way. It was the Pastor's life endowment to the members that they share in twelve Masses to be offered during every year of the organization's activity.

"Eighty-five members were enrolled at that first meeting. The officers elected that day were:

Spiritual Director.................................Father Edward J. McGolrick
President ....Miss J. I. Clarkson
Secretary ....Miss Gertrude Vaughan
Secretary ....Mrs. M. E. Golden

The present officers are:

Spiritual Director ....Rt. Rev. Monsignor McGolrick
President...Mrs. S. A. Darrow
Vice-President ....Mrs. J. Butler
Treasurer ....Mrs. W. Duff
Secretary ....Mrs. M. E. Golden

The children are in charge of Miss Mary McCormack as Matron."

The Day Nursery Opened.

"The Day Nursery was opened on St. Cecilia's Day in the year 1904. It's first home was the reading room of the Lyceum, with Mrs. Bollinger as Matron. Approximately twenty children were registered that day. William Glinnen, M. D. volunteered to look after the physical well-being of the little ones. At his demise this most important work was taken up by Edward V. McGoldrick, M. D.

"In 1905, the Nursery moved its quarters to 25 Monitor Street, where more room and better housing facilities were available.

"In 1917, a Building Fund was started, and in 1922 the Association had on hand $7,000. This amount was turned over to the Pastor to enable him to purchase a new building. In June of that year the commodius residence at 210 Richardson Street was converted into a Nursery. On November 9, the thirty-fourth anniversary of the Pastor's coming to St. Cecilia's parish, the Nursery began a new and better life in the larger and more thoroughly equipped home.

"During the history of the Nursery, a Mr. Isaac Fluegelman was a great benefactor. His contributions of food and toys brought much happiness to the children. When the Nursery moved into its p r e s e n t home, Mr. Fluegelman generously contributed furnishings for kitchen, dining-room, meeting-room. He also had electricity installed throughout the house.

"The Nursery cares for about thirty-five children daily. Maintenance is carried on by the Association."

The Secretary's report makes no mention of the essential reason actuating the Pastor in the establishment of a parish Day Nursery.

A well-intentioned society with purpose to care for the physical needs and to direct the moral training of children of the very poor in certain sections of Brooklyn bought a plot of ground in close proximity to St. Cecilia's Church. They erected thereon a three story brick building to be known as "Settlement House" and a very commodious dwelling to house the little ones of a Day Nursery. In due course, the Society opened its doors. The Pastor of St. Cecilia's spoke of the adventure from his pulpit and, in neighborly spirit, gave his blessing to the charitable intent of the undertaking, wishing for it all success within its own sphere.

There was at the same time in the Pastor's mind a vivid consciousness of the ill effects which might come to the needy children of his own parish through the zealous work of the Society. Such effects he was vigilant to forestall.

For the Catholic, moral training rests upon a very firm foundation, namely, the proper relationship of man to his God and to his fellow-creatures for love of God. This foundation impaired, moral training has no stability; this foundation away, moral training has no meaning. It may become merely a matter of expediency, a matter of doing what is approved by society for society's approval and the individual's profitable rank therein. Whenever, then, the moral training of children is involved, the Catholic Pastor must be alert to the security of the foundation upon which such training purports to rest.

Immediately, the Pastor of St. Cecilia's called a meeting of the women of the parish. The purpose and conduct of that initial meeting is given in the Secretary's report printed above. The women were filled with enthusiasm for the furtherance of the Pastor's project, namely, the establishment of such a Day Nursery as would care for the physical wants of needy children in the parish and would at the same time safeguard their moral-training.

Inspired by the leadership of their pastor and blessed by the Masses offered in their behalf, the ladies of the St. Cecilia's

Day Nursery Association set about a great good work. A work, it is, that not only takes care of the child's body but also ministers unto his soul. There is wisdom and truth in the old saying—"As the twig is bent, the tree is inclined." The Supreme Judge alone can fully measure what evil inclination is spared the coming man or woman by keeping the tiny tot removed from bad companions and harmful play. This the Day Nursery is doing. Moreover, at a cost of only ten cents per day, an additional number of school children are provided a wholesome noon-day meal. Working mothers are thus, through the efforts of the Day Nursery, given practical assistance in the rearing of their babies.

For about sixteen years the Settlement House and Day Nursery of the "Brooklyn Industrial School Society" functioned in the Greenpoint section. Then they closed their doors and buildings, which had cost the Society eighty-five thousand dollars, went into disuse. For two year both buildings remained untenanted, save by the caretaker.

Meanwhile, the members of St. Cecilia's Association were carrying on their good work with unabated enthusiasm. They had moved into their Monitor Street quarters and had purchased a lot for sixteen hundred dollars, with intent to build a better home thereon. But, when bids were obtained the lowest bid was staggering, fifty-four thousand dollars. The Society could not assume this financial responsibility. However, a ray of light brightened the horizon. One of the members had been making judicious inquiry and reported to the Pastor that she believed the long vacant buildings of the Brooklyn Industrial School Society could be purchased at bargain price.

The project seemed promising. Earnest effort was directed toward its consummation, and soon thereafter the two substantial buildings which had cost so much passed into the possession of St. Cecilia's parish for the surprisingly low figure of forty thousand dollars. The blessing which the pastor had extended from the pulpit years before seemed indeed to have acted like the scriptural story of bread cast upon the waters.

The Day Nursery building was at once taken over by the St. Cecilia Day Nursery. What use was to be made of the "Settlement Building" appears elsewhere in this parish record.

Referring again to the Secretary's report, there is mention therein of the benefactions of one Isaac Fluegelman. Here was a real friend to St. Cecilia's Day Nursery, a large hearted friend to the little ones it shelters. The poet sings:

> "Who gives himself with his gift feeds three,
> Himself, his hungering neighbor and ME."

Mr. Fluegelman's giving was of this type. For eight or ten years he not only supplied the Thanksgiving Feast for the children in the Nursery but came himself to carve the turkeys and to feast his heart in watching the children's joy. Nor did he discontinue this generous practise when he had moved from the neighborhood into New York. Even then he came with his gifts each Thanksgiving Day and Christmas until Death summoned him home. All the more generous does his action appear when we consider that he was not a member of the parish not a believer in the Catholic faith. He was a Jew who greatly admired the Church's care for the helpless little ones. O, may it be that in such giving this busy business man stored up for himself rich treasure where "moth and rust consume not."

What thinking mind does not admire the consistency of the Church's teachings and practices looking to the rights of childhood. From the instant of conception Holy Mother Church recognizes and defends the child's rights, the right to life, to baptism, to Christian education. She insists, with all a true mother's tender devotion, that nothing dare stand in the way of these rights—neither ill health, extreme poverty, excessive wealth, no, nor the forbidding frown of worldly fashion.

St. Cecilia's Day Nursery is one of the first best charities found within a parish rich in charitable activities. It is in keeping with the Church's spirit, the spirit of justice and mercy. Its presence among them doubtless calls down manifold blessings upon the people of St. Cecilia's.

SILVER JUBILEE CELEBRATION

1882—1907.

The members of the general committee in charge of preparations for the celebration of the Silver Jubilee of the ordination of Father McGolrick were:

James F. Fitzpatrick, chairman; Hon. Owen J. Murphy, Hon. Edward Glinnen, Hon. Daniel Collins, Joseph J. Schulte, Charles Skehan, John L. Moore, Joseph E. Reydel, James L. Flynn, Wm. P. Murphy, Harry McGill, Adam Eich, John J. Byrne, Bernard Daily, Joseph Golden, William Ward, Joseph Henschell, Thomas J. Kelly, Rev. James F. Irwin.

The committee in charge of the Souvenir Brochure on that occasion was composed of Rev. James Irwin, Peter Kelleher and Henry McGill.

1882   1907

Souvenir of the

Silver Jubilee of

Rev. Edward J. McGolrick

Rector and Builder of

St. Cecilia's Church

North Henry and Herbert Streets

Brooklyn, N. Y.

OUR PASTOR

"By the grace of God I am what I am . . . a priest forever."

I Cor. xv. 10.

REV. FATHER McGOLRICK.

Monday, June 3d, 1907, has come, and the people of St. Cecilia's Parish, Brooklyn, are happy, for it witnesses the twenty-fifth mile-stone in the priestly life of their Pastor, Rev. E. J. McGolrick. The occasion is one which will not soon be forgotten. The joy of the young and old, the rich and poor, is unconfined. Their heartiest and best wishes for his welfare in the future and their sincerest congratulations on the completion of his twenty-five years of priestly labors are laid at his feet.

This Souvenir is a token of esteem from a united and grateful congregation to a much beloved pastor. The committee commissioned to bring it to the light of day, regard it as a work of love and trust that it will serve to increase the affection and devotion of all who read it for him whom we honor to-day.

In the name of the people of St. Cecilia's we offer a hearty congratulation to the Jubilarian. Twenty-five years of fruitful work in a happy vineyard is certainly a mark of great distinction. We assure him that his labors and sacrifices are appreciated by all. We know that in his hands the interests of religion and the influences for good exerted by Catholic teachings and practices have prospered and the lives of all in communication with St. Cecilia's have largely benefited by his zealous labors and unselfish industry.

May God in His wisdom see fit to keep him amongst us for many years to come. May the blessings of God remain with him and prosper him in all his plans for the future and may the happiness of a long life, a fruitful ministry and ripe old age, full of sweet memories be his, is the wish and hope of his loving and grateful congregation.

Committee, James F. Irwin,
Peter Kelleher,
Henry McGill.

FATHER McGOLRICK—AN APPRECIATION.

Rev. Edward J. McGolrick was born in Ireland, on May 9th, 1857. He was brought to this city when very young, and received his early education at St. James School, on Jay Street, Brooklyn. His collegiate course was made at Manhattan College, New York City, graduating with honors in the class of 1877. Resolving to devote his life to the church he proceeded at once to the American College at Rome and there, amidst the historic environments of the Holy City, he spent five years in study and was ordained priest at the church of St. John Lateran by His Eminence, Cardinal Monaco La Valetta, on June 3rd, 1882. In the words of a dear friend and companion, "during his years of study at the American College, he was distinguished for his constant good humor and kindly bearing toward all. It is remembered to this day by his companions that not an unpleasant word ever escaped him and that he never exhibited any of those breaks in temper that are so common among the young and inexperienced. His devotion to study was irreproachable, and he always stood well in the examinations and competitions that marked the close of the year's study in the Propaganda College. He was particularly beloved by the students of the other English-speaking colleges (the Irish, English and the Scotch), who never failed to seek him out when they met the American students, in any of the

FATHER McGOLRICK AS A STUDENT AT THE AMERICAN COLLEGE, ROME

Roman villas that were then, as now, the haunts of young ecclesiastics during their hours of recreation. He was even then a man of solid principle and perfect honor, in whom all his juniors were wont to confide, and whom all his superiors considered every way trustworthy and exemplary."

After his ordination, Father McGolrick made a tour of Europe, and on his return home was assigned by the late Bishop Loughlin to a curacy at St. Patrick's parish where he remained working hard and faithfully for six years until he was appointed rector of St. Cecilia's church. On November 9, 1888, he succeeded Father Malone at St. Cecilia's and began to face as discouraging a situation as ever befell the lot of a young priest in the city. The so-called parochial residence was a place unfit to live in and the poor wooden church was encumbered with a debt of about $5,000. Many of the parishioners were either going to neighboring churches or to no church at all. Father McGolrick set about his work with a courageous heart and devised ways and means for the good of the parish. Soon the policy adopted by him of interesting the men and their societies, succeeded, and the "day's pay plan," so well know to us all, paid off the debt and enabled him to begin the work of erecting the beautiful new St. Cecilia's the corner-stone of which was laid on September 27, 1891.

The feat of erecting St. Cecilia's Church and Rectory and having it solemnly consecrated within twelve years, at a cost of over $200,000, is truly regarded as one of the most remarkable in parish management in the history of the diocese, or of the country, and considering that at all times the bulk of the parishioners was made up of the working classes, we feel that after the strong impulses of divine faith it was mainly the result of a sincere and appreciative love on their part for the pastor who ministered so well the things of God in their behalf.

The next great work was the erection of the now well known Rt. Rev. John Loughlin Memorial Lyceum, a modern institution elegantly fitted up with a complete equipment for dramatic, social, educational, and physical culture efforts. Its yearly calendar is a complete circuit of gala and joyous gatherings where priest and people meet and the young and old come together for social enjoyment and incidentally, to benefit the various objects of sweet charity.

The needs of the poor and of the young have been the special object of Father McGolrick's endeavors at St. Cecilia's. The Kindergarten with its bright classes of youngsters learning their first lessons from a devoted teacher, was the first step made in the direction of Catholic education, to be perfected with the opening of the new St. Cecilia's school. The

ST. CECILIA CHURCH

Day Nursery with its happy family of helpless tots brought each morning to the loving arms of the matron, is a blessing much appreciated by all, but especially by the poor, hardworking mothers who are free from all care when they know that the children are enjoying the hospitality of the St. Cecilia's Day Nursery. No labor is too great, no expense too heavy for Father McGolrick when it is a question of providing for the poor children entrusted to him. The military organization, the Loughlin Battalion, so well known in Brooklyn, came next, and together with the Drum, Fife and Bugle Corps, they are the pride of the younger generation of the section and the admiration of the "grown ups." For twenty years, Major John L. Moore, gave three hours weekly of his time, gratuitously, to the training of the boys of the Battalion. The Battalion was invited to take part in the parade escorting the New York 69th Regiment to its new armory. *The New York Herald,* on the following morning said, "that the Loughlin Battalion marched with the precision of West Point Cadets."

The great work of building the new St. Cecilia's Parochial School is the crowning effort of his nineteen years in the midst of us. The occasion of the Jubilee shows the magnificent pile rearing itself high in the air awaiting the finishing touches that will complete it and make of it the finest parochial school building in Brooklyn. The cost of the school will be in the neighborhood of $200,000. Every effort for the past few years has had the benefit of the school in view. No work appeals more to Catholic people to-day than the work of Catholic education, which will supply for the children of the future a solid foundation of faith and morals that will enable them to resist the growing spirit of lawlessness so rampant to-day. The generosity of his people and the universal good-will of all show that with heart and soul the parishioners are united with Father McGolrick to a man, and wish him every success in his

work. And now that the great day is at hand when he cele-
brates his Silver Jubilee, the people of St. Cecilia's, without
consultation with him, are spending every effort to make it an
occasion long to be remembered. His place in the affections
of all is strong and fixed. For they realize and appreciate how
great a blessing has been theirs in having his guiding hand so
long directing their affairs, for to all it is evident that the
promises of his early manhood have reached a perfect matur-
ity at St. Cecilia's, and "It may be said with truth that he was
never varied in character from the days of his early priesthood; rather has he gone on developing the excellent qualities inherited from an admirable father and an equally admirable mother.

His early ambition was to be a good priest of the Catholic
Church, and he has accomplished in no slight degree his holy
ambition. The interests of the church and the people have been
at all times his guiding star. What seemed to him their welfare was a law to him, no matter how great or how constant
the sacrifices. To this unbroken devotion he has added qualities of prudence and perseverance that are household words
amongst his people. He has been their leader in spiritual
things as all gladly testify. In the long hours of the confessional, in the laborious and varied work of Sunday and holy-
day, in visiting the sick and comforting the poor, in the im-
parting of advice and encouraging the distracted, in the de-
fense of the helpless and the oppressed, he has at all times
been found at his proper place, and has always measured up
to the full requirements of his high office. While faithful
always to the discipline of the church, he has been ingenious
and progressive in his attempts to lighten and vary the heavy
burdens of his parishioners and to render pleasant and easy
for them the material growth of their beautiful church property. As an administrator of ecclesiastical revenues and

goods he has exhibited all due fidelity, caution and attention. Year by year his people have witnessed the increase of their holdings, the improvement of the church services, the perfection of all the surroundings, the careful vigilance over the entire property of St. Cecilia's. If they have given generously they cannot deny that the Lord has sent them a faithful, intelligent and affectionate steward in whose hands their talents have multiplied enormously. Father McGolrick is especially the friend of the young. He has always kept in mind not only their spiritual welfare, but also their temporal happiness. Few churches in the United States can boast so complete a provision for all the needs of youth in a city parish. He believes that the battle of Catholic faith is to be won through the affections no less than the intellect and that if the boys and girls of the parish grow up loving the surroundings of the church. If they can never remember a time when the church, their church, was anything but a loving mother, they will not stray very far from her in their mature years."

God bless him, then, the man, the priest, and the pastor; may he live to celebrate his Golden Jubilee with his beloved flock; may he ever increase in fervor and zeal, and may he ever receive alike the final commendation of his work from a grateful people and a crown of bliss from Him whose work he is doing so well.

THE IDEAL PARISH PRIEST.
(A True Picture)

"There is a man in every parish, who, having no family, belongs to a family that is world-wide; who is called in as a witness, a counsellor and an actor in all the most important affairs of civil life. No one comes into the world or goes hence without his ministrations. He takes the child from the arms of his mother and parts with him only at the grave. He blesses and consecrates the cradle, the bridal chamber, the bed of death and the bier. He is one whom innocent children grow to love, to venerate and to reverence; whom even those who know him not salute as *Father;* at whose feet Christians fall down and lay bare the inmost thoughts of their souls and weep their most sacred tears. He is one whose mission is to console the afflicted and soften the pains of body and soul; who is an intermediary between the affluent and the indigent; to whose door come alike the rich and the poor—the rich to give alms in secret, and the poor to receive them without blushing. He belongs to no social class, because he belongs equally to all— to the lower by his poverty and not unfrequently by his humble birth; to the upper by his culture and his knowledge, and by the elevated sentiments which a religion, itself all charity, inspires and imposes. He is one, in fine, who knows all, has a right to speak unreservedly, and whose speech, inspired from on high, falls on the minds and hearts of all with the authority of one who is divinely sent, and with the constraining power of one who has an unclouded faith.

"Such is the parish priest, than whom no one has a greater opportunity for good or power or evil, accordingly as he fulfils or fails to recognize his transcendent mission among men."

REV. JAMES F. IRWIN

REV. MARTIN BIGGANE   REV. JOSE REVERA

ORDER OF SERVICES

Solemn High Mass, Monday, June 3rd, 10:30 A. M.

Rt. Rev. Charles E. McDonnell, D. D., Presiding
Celebrant, Rev. Edward J. McGolrick   Deacon, Rev. James F. Irwin
Sub-Deacon, Rev. Jose de las Mercedes Revera

Masters of Ceremonies
Rev. Martin F. Biggane   Rev. Thomas Connolly   Mr. Charles A. Rohr
Sermon Delivered by Rev. John E. Burke

PROGRAM OF MUSIC

Prelude—Allegro ....*Beethoven*
Organ and Orchestra

KYRIE—Gounod's St. Cecilia Mass

GLORIA—Mozart's 12th Mass

OFFERTORY—Tues Sacerdos ....*Hayden*

CREDO—Gounod's St. Cecilia Mass

SANCTUS—Gounod's St. Cecilia Mass

BENEDICTUS—Gounod's St. Cecilia Mass

AGNUS DEI—Gounod's St. Cecilia Mass

POSTLUDE—Priests' March ....*Mendelssohn*

SOLOISTS—Miss Anna Solan ....*Soprano*
Mrs. John Thiery ....*Alto*
Mr. James O'Niel ....*Tenor*
Mrs. George McGourty ....*Bass*

CHORUS OF EIGHTY AND ORCHESTRA

Louis Hannweber, Organist

THE PASTOR AND HIS BOYS

GRAND MILITARY AND CIVIC DEMONSTRATION

in honor of

The Silver Jubilee of Rev. Edward J. McGolrick

Pastor of St. Cecilia's Church

ON MONDAY EVENING, JUNE 3, 1907

Major John L. Moore, Grand Marshal

PARADE FORMATION

McAuliff's Military Band

Loughlin Drum, Fife and Bugle Corps

Catholic Boys Brigade—Col. Wm. J. Crawford, Commandant.

Leo Battalion and Loughlin Battalion composing Brigade

First New York Regiment Knights of Columbus—Uniformed

F. F. Williams' Drum, Fife and Bugle Corps

F. F. Williams' Battery—Commandant F. F. Williams

Invited guests in carriages

St. Cecilia's Holy Name Society

St. Anthony's Holy Name Society

St. Aloysius Sodality of St. Cecilia

Herbert Council Catholic Benevolent Legion

Ancient Order of Hibernians of Kings County,

  P. J. McCarthy, Marshal

Grand Divisions

Councils of Catholic Benevolent Legion

Councils of Knights of Columbus

Holy Name Societies of St. Mary's, St. Vincent de Paul's, St.

  Stanislaus and Holy Rosary parishes

Civic Societies and Organizations.

PUBLIC RECEPTION TO FATHER McGOLRICK

TUESDAY EVENING, JUNE 4, 1907
AT LOUGHLIN LYCEUM

On the Occasion of His Silver Jubilee

Tendered by the Parishioners and Parish Organizations

Orchestra under direction of Mr. Louis Hanweber

Choruses from Large Choir and Children's Choir

ADDRESSES

1 A Voice from the Nursery—
2 A Word from the Kindergarten—
3 Angels Sodality...Miss Pratt
4 St. Aloysius ....Master Rakers
5 Woman's C. B. L..Miss Annie Worden
6 Loughlin Battalion ....Major George Leonard
7 Children of Mary...Miss Kate Kelly
8 Reading Circle ....Miss Ormond
9 Loughlin Lyceum ....Mr. Harry McGill
10 Holy Name ....Mr. Patrick Boylan
11 The Parish ....Rev. James F. Irwin
12 Response—The Jubilarian ....Rev. Edward J. McGolrick

MUSIC

General Committee: James F. Fitzpatrick, Chairman; Hon.
Owen J. Murphy, Hon. Edw. Glinnen, Hon. Daniel Collins,
Joseph J. Schutta, Charles Skehan, John L. Moore, Joseph E.
Reydel, James L. Flynn, Wm. P. Murphy, Harry McGill, Adam
Eich, John J. Byrne, Bernard Daily, Joseph Golden, William
Ward, Joseph Henschel, Thos. J. Kelly, David Acker, James
Canning, Edward Carroll, Wm. H. Thornton, John F. Kelly.
John J. Schutta, Rev. James F. Irwin.

ST. CECILIA'S PAROCHIAL SCHOOL.

(Primary and Grammar Grades)

After the Church itself, nothing is more important in any parish than its school. Our Lord counseled: "Suffer the little children to come unto Me." In the Catholic school, children come unto a knowledge and love of their faith, the faith that springs from and leads to Christ. Physical and intellectual education is never neglected nor slighted but there is added a daily training in faith and morals vitally necessary to the heart of the child if he is thru life to be a loyal and worthy citizen of his country and in death an inheritor of the kingdom of Heaven.

When the child is thoroughly grounded in his religion, he is able to intelligently explain it to the honest enquirer or to defend it against the vilifier. Moreover, in this age of infidelity the recesses of his own heart have stored away in them Divine truths to strengthen and stabilize erring nature against the anti-religious trend of the times.

The year 1908 is memorable in the history of the parish, for then it was that the new St. Cecilia's school opened its doors. Children of the first six grades were enrolled that year but very soon the seventh and eighth grades were added.

The building is a large and solid structure of pressed brick with ornate facade. It was built at a cost of $240,000.00. It stands at the corner of Monitor and Richardson Streets. From its iron-railed roof garden, an excellent survey of the Greenpoint section is gained. Elevators are installed.

I was intensely interested throughout my all too brief visit. I found myself looking at the building and classes from the school-teacher's viewpoint, a viewpoint I thought I had forgotten. Broad halls with cement flooring, double stairways at either end of the building, numerous exits, excellent fire-

ST. CECILIA SCHOOL
Dedicated September 13th, 1908

escapes. "Splendid!" said the teacher in me. "Little ones pretty safe here even if fire should break out. Rooms well lighted, desks so placed as to reduce eye strain. Fine!"

"I want you to meet our nurse," said Sister M. Oswald, Principal of the Girls' School.

"Nurse?"

"Yes, we have a regular nurse who attends to the pupils in both the boys' and girls' schools. Miss Meany has been in charge for the past three or four years. She knows the children very well, knows their home conditions, their general health tendencies, etc. And she knows her work. We have a visiting Physician also. In this way, the physical condition of each and every child is watched very carefully and we are able to offset or at least to check the spread of contagious diseases."

"Health reports are made each day so also are truant reports."

"What system of discipline prevails," I asked.

"The Honor System obtains in both schools."

At the mention of the Honor System the first flash of my thought was resentful for there are strange contradictions in our age—the tendency to grant youth uncurbed freedom and to impose upon age the arbitrary restrictions born of fanaticism. Intently now I eyed the conduct of the children. In every class room they were diligently and quietly pursuing their studies. I watched them as they formed for dismissal—twenty-one hundred pupils or more, the largest Parochial Grammar School in the Brooklyn diocese or indeed in any diocese in the country. The order was impressive not only in its line formation and within the halls of the school, but without as well.

I began to realize the secret of the success of the Honor System in vogue here. On Honor System backed by daily lessons in morals and religion does not cater to the evil of uncurbed freedom. In the child's understanding are firmly fixed the individual's power of free will and the ten commandments of Almighty God. In his own way, he knows that no more in youth than in age dare his freedom be uncurbed. He himself must curb it to meet the requirements of the Supreme Law or he must suffer eternal consequences under the sentence of the most scrutible and just Judge.

All this does not mean that there is no youthful offender found in St. Cecilia's School. Far from it. But it does mean that religion alone—that is the moral responsibility of the individual to recognize and obey the Supreme Law Giver—is the only true corrective force in the world. Religion cast aside, crime and chaos enter.

In the Girls' School, Social Etiquette is included in the Physical Training classes. I talked with Sister Oswald over the changed ways in today's classroom and was particularly interested in the up-to-the-minute methods in reading which are employed in St. Cecilia's.

Though the Boys' and Girls' Schools are housed in the one building they are conducted separately. The Sisters of St. Joseph having charge of the girls' classes and the Christian Brothers the boys. There are twenty-four lay teachers.

In each school the entire time of the Principal is devoted to supervision of classes, inspection of lesson plans, report work, teachers' meetings, etc. There are visiting supervisors as well.

It was Sister Grace Winifred whom the Principal graciously assigned to accompany me through the Girls' department. She explained that no one was more qualified to answer all my questions for Sister Grace Winifred had come with the pioneer group and was the only one of that group still teaching in St. Cecilia's.

The pupils are of Irish, Polish, Italian and German extraction. There has been a gradual lessening of the number of

Irish children and an increase of the Polish and Italian element in the district.

Diocesan and Regents examinations are conducted twice a year. St. Cecilia's is a Regents centre, that is, pupils from seventh and eighth grades in other buildings assemble here for examination. The Diocesan examinations follow the Regents in January and precede them in June. All grades are required to pass the Diocesan examinations. These are sent out by the Superintendent of Brooklyn Catholic Schools, the Rev. Joseph McClancy.

Commencement exercises take place in the Church twice each year, and are of a solemn and impressive character. The graduates are addressed by the Pastor or some invited clergyman. Benediction follows. The music during Benediction hour is furnished by the seventh grade boys at one commencement and by the girls of the same grade the next.

Sister led me to the Principal's office in the Boys' School and parted with me there, promising to conduct me thru the Convent during the noon hour.

Brother Victor was in charge at the time. He is now pursuing a course in Ascetic Theology in the Mother House of the Christian Brothers, at Lembecq-Lez-Hal, Belgium. A letter recently received from him by the Pastor appears elsewhere in the book. Brother Conrad has succeeded to his office of Principal of the Boys' School and Director of the Monastery.

I recall how enthusiastic Brother Victor grew when speaking of the Athletic triumphs of St. Cecilia's boys. For five years they carried off all basket-ball and track work honors in the "Catholic Schools Athletic League." This League includes athletes from the twenty-five or more schools taught by the Christian Brothers in Greater New York.

It was a sight worth witnessing to watch the hundreds of pupils march out of the building and to note the order kept by the lines. The teachers of the Primary grades, to guard the tiny tots from automobile accidents, accompany their classes to the street corners where policemen are waiting to follow out the good work.

ST. CECILIA'S SCHOOL.
Girls' Department

The Pioneer group of Sisters: Sr. St. Luke, Sr. M. Irene, Sr. M. Ursula, Sr. Grace Winifred, Sr. M. Theotine, Sr. Thomas Anna, Sr. Natalie.

The Sisters who have served as Principals of the School and Superiors of the Convent, from 1908 to 1930: Sr. St. Luke, Sr. M. Raymondina, Sr. Joseph Pius, Sr. M. Oswald, Sr. M. Inez,

The Present Teaching Staff: Sr. M. Patrice, Sr. M. Rosalie, Sr. Grace Winifred, Sr. St. Hugh, Sr. M. Collette, Sr. M. Gonzalva, Sr. M. Simeon Josephine, Sr. Concepta Maria, Sr. M. Teresa de Lourdes, Sr. M. Anastasius, Sr. M. Teresa Josephine, Sr. Alice Marie, Sr. M. Margaret Gertrude, Sr. M. Frances Stephanie, Sr. Consuela Marie, Sr. M. Norbert, Miss Nellie Phillips, Mrs. Rose Kelly, Miss Catherine Schutte, Miss Mary Long.

ST. CECILIA'S SCHOOL.
Boys' Department

Principals of the School and Directors of the Monastery: Brother Binen Michael 1908-1912; Brother Arnulf Paul 1912-1916; Brother Austin Julian 1916-1919; Brother Anselm Emilious 1919-1924; Brother Eliphus Victor 1924-1930.

Present Staff: Brother Conrad, Brother Nicholas, Brother Joseph, Brother Leo, Brother Charles, Brother James, Brother Andrew, Mrs. Anna Turner, Mrs. Anna Durkin, Mrs. McGinn, Mrs. Bealer, Miss Taggart, Miss N. Lefante, Mrs. McHugh, Miss O'Bryan, Mrs. Schmitt, Miss Margaret Byrne, Miss Dorothy Golden, Miss Augusta Segreto, Miss McGlatz.

THE GRADUATES.

Every Commencement has for its essence sadness for always the occasion is haunted by the future's uncertainty. Where will these boys and girls go? How will they end their days?

It is not possible to trace the footsteps of every graduate. However, I did glean a few interesting facts concerning the pupils who have gone out from St. Cecilia's School. To begin with, the graduates of the Girls' School have a loyal Alumnae Association. They meet once a month and once a year they receive Holy Communion in a body and enjoy an after Communion breakfast in the Loughlin Lyceum. To every enterprise of the parish, "St. Cecilia's Alumnae Association" has given generous support.

About fifty of the girls have entered the St. Joseph Sisterhood. This certainly reflects credit on the nuns who have taught in the school. Other graduates now belong to the Sisters of Mercy, to the Maryknoll Sisters devoted to Foreign Missionary Work, to the Good Shepherds, the Dominicans and the Carmelites. A number are very successful teachers in the public schools of Brooklyn and New York. And the Baptistery records of the parish show that not a few of them are now good mothers who have more than one interest in St. Cecilia's Parochial School.

The boys, too, can give an excellent account of themselves. There are priests among them—priests in various orders. Two, at least, of these are engaged in Missionary work in China. Others, drawn thereto by the example of their teachers at St. Cecilia's and Manhattan as well, have become Christian Brothers.

Boys of the parish who have been called to the priesthood during the pastorate of Monsignor McGolrick are:—

Very Rev. Msgr. Edward Hoare, President, Diocesan Seminary, Huntington, L. I.;

Rev. Thomas Connolly, Pastor, St. Mary's, East Islip, L. I.;

Rev. William Daley, Secretary to Bishop Molloy;

Rev. Aloysius Gillick, Pastor, Imm. Conception, Bayport, L. I.;

Rev. Clarence E. Murphy, Pastor, St. James, L. I.;

Rev. Bernard Reilly, Pastor of Our Lady of Lourdes, Queens Village, L. I.;

Rev. Ch. A. Rohr, Pastor, St. Lawrence Church, Sayville, L. I.;

Rev. Wm. Duhigg, deceased;

Rev. Father Fidelis, O. F. M.;

Rev. Philip Taggert, M. M. China Mission, China;

Rev. Quentin Olwell, C. S. P., China Mission, China;

Rev. Peter Keleher, St. Athanasius Church, Brooklyn;

Rev. John Keenan, D. J. C., C. M., Germantown, Pa.;

Rev. Francis Keenan, C. M., Niagara University;

Rev. Henry Hald, Assistant Inspector of Schools;

Rev. Peter Jessup, St. Mary's, Long Island City;

Rev. George Helfenstein, St. Augustine's, Brooklyn;

Rev. Martin Treacy, Diocese of Syracuse;

Rev. Thos. Burke, Diocese of Newark;

Rev. John O'Brien, St. Thomas Aquinas, Brooklyn;

Rev. William Rickert, St. Mary Magdalene, Springfield, L. I.;

Rev. Thomas Kelly, Rome, Italy;

Rev. Thos. McGee, Rome, Italy.

THE DE LA SALLE MONASTERY.

At the corner of Richardson and North Henry Streets, stands the parish home of the Christian Brothers who teach in the Boys' School. There are seven members in the community and Brother Conrad is the Director.

The Monastery is a two-story brick building of recent construction. Within a niche over the front entrance stands a white marble statue of the Founder of the Order of Christian Brothers, Saint John Baptist de La Salle. I did not visit the Monastery.

Elsewhere in this book, an abler pen than mine has described the character and noble work of the Christian Brothers. The Pastor of St. Cecilia's has chosen them for teachers in this parish because of his own certain knowledge of their teaching power, gleaned in his Manhattan days. There is nothing I can add to such encomiums.

LETTER FROM BROTHER E. VICTOR.

Institut des Freres des Ecoles Chretiennes.
Maison Saint-Joseph,
Lembecq-lez-Hal, Belgique.   Le November 1, 1930.
Dear Monsignor:

I was very sorry to hear about your injury. Since that time I have been praying each day for your swift and complete recovery. To one as active as you are, the occasion must be annoying. Yet, I feel, with your sterling faith you have accepted the cross sent to you.

As an outstanding affiliated member of the Brothers of the Christian Schools, I'm sure you'll be interested to hear something concerning Lembecq.

It is the Mother House of our order. Here reside the Superior General and his twelve assistants. In addition there are three departments; a small novitiate, a large novitiate, and our group of second novices. The first two form what is termed an apostolic group, for, on the completion of their preparatory studies, these young Brothers are sent to foreign missions.

We number sixty-four and represent fifteen nations. French is the common means of communication, and for the conferences. Our big job here is to make a study of the science of Ascetic Theology and to make a practical application of it in our lives by following the example of our founder, St. John Baptist De La Salle.

I'm trying to reap all the benefit possible from the splendid chance which has been afforded me. I'm most certain I have your prayers for this aim.

News from the Brothers and the boys of St. Cecilia's keeps me in touch with things Cecilian. I'm pleased everything is moving along in splendid shape. You can rest assured many parts of the world where Christian Brothers are, know about the large parochial school in Greenpoint. They are amazed to hear of a Catholic school housing twenty-two hundred children. And when I spoke of the numerous other activities carried on in the parish, they were startled. You certainly have built a monument; something as an example of what can be done when there is constant, zealous sacrifice for Christ.

May I ask you to accept at this early date my sincere wishes for a blessed Christmastide, and a Happy New Year, replete with choice graces.

Extend, if you will, my good wishes to your assistants.

Yours in J. M. J.,

Brother E. Victor.

ST. CECILIA'S CONVENT.

The Convent home of the St. Joseph nuns, who teach in St. Cecilia's school, is located next door to the school on Monitor Street. It is a substantial and impressive three story building of ornate facade. In a wall niche above the front bay and beneath the building's surmounting cross, stands a statue of St. Cecilia, patron of the parish.

The eight Sisters, who were first to come to minister to the intellectual needs of the little girls in St. Cecilia's parish, had other and less comfortable dwelling place. For four years, they made their home in the rooms on the top floor of the school building. In 1912, they moved into the present commodious Convent home and their vacated quarters made it possible to increase the number of class rooms in the school and admit thereto seventh and eighth grade pupils.

In some respects, a Convent home is a lonesome one. Its inhabitants are separated from father and mother, from sister and brother. In willing self-denial they dwell apart from their loved ones to devote all their time to the service of God. In Community life, they may not choose their companions. They are daily associated with fellow workers who may be of alien race or nature and yet, they are not privileged to offer complaint nor establish favoritism. The Rule which governs their life-dedication to the sole service of Christ, their Master, emphasizes the virtue of self-renouncement and forbids the indulgence of any form of selfishness. The more noble the nun, the more earnestly she struggles to fulfill this Rule. Each nun is assigned for her own cell, only a plain little room furnished with bed, table or desk, and a straight wooden chair. On the wall of each room is hung a crucifix, perpetual reminder of Christ's supreme self-sacrifice and His uncomplaining suffer-

ST. CECILIA CONVENT

ing. Outside of actual teaching hours, the Sisters dwell in community life, working or studying together. Their recreative hours also are spent for the most part in the community room and the daily rule of life sets aside certain hours for community prayers. The home in so far may be considered lonesome.

But say now, is it? There is in every Convent a very special room and in it abides a very Special Friend to each and all of them. He knows the sorrows of each heart; He understands the weakness of each nature; He sees, with truer vision than could the most loving of mothers or fathers, the real self of the child. He sees not the act alone, but the intent behind it; He hears not the word only but the silent thought; He knows the secret nagging of the flesh to break the spirit down. In short, He knows and understands the full self of every dweller in the house. The door of His room is never locked. He waits to comfort and console.

It is to the King's room that Sister Grace Winifred led me when I entered the Convent home. The name of His room is the Chapel and in the Tabernacle there He is silently enthroned. What a beautiful Chapel, the Sisters of St. Joseph have in their home on Monitor Street. And how the hours spent therein must soothe away the secret heartaches and trials of community life. The parishioners have been most generous in meeting the Pastor's plans for the Chapel's embellishment. I cannot recall the names of all the donors of windows, statues, stations and other furnishings of the lovely room of the Convent's Special Dweller, so I shall refrain from mentioning any. I do, however, very vividly remember the beauty of their gifts.

The entire interior of the building has recently been redecorated and the cleanliness, which ever and always pervades a Convent, seemed more than ever pronounced at St. Cecilia's when I visited there.

In the Reception room, there is a triptych, representing the Annunciation, Visitation and Nativity. This oil painting was executed under the training of Sister M. Albertine, by Sister M. Consuela, who was in girlhood, a member of the parish.

Sister M. Inez is the present Superior and there are sixteen Sisters under her care. Their very special Feast day is St. Joseph's and so on the nineteenth of March, the Girls' School is closed.

The Mother House of the Community is located at Brentwood, Long Island. A number of the graduates of St. Cecilia's Grammar School pursue their High School course at St. Joseph's Academy in Brentwood.

THE ST. CECILIA LIBRARY.

The St. Cecilia Library is located on Monitor Street next door to the Convent. Miss Mary Kekut is in charge. Books may be drawn by the children during the day hours. The evening hours are devoted to grown-up patronage.

The old saying, "Show me your company and I'll tell you what you are," has in it more truth than fiction. In Bookland live the good or evil thoughts of good or evil people. We may say then, "Show me what books you read and I'll tell you what you are."

It is a serious obligation resting on every Catholic to do all that he can to protect young minds against the insidious evil of bad books. From a flesh and blood bad companion one may separate the child but, from the thought pictures left by a bad book, who has the power to separate him?

Nowadays, when vile reading matter is turned out in carloads, when its filth is dressed alluringly, when it is so easily accessible to the young, how constant and tactful must parents and teachers be in their vigilance against its vitiating influence.

So, the parish that has for one of its activities the conduct of a Library as extensive and well-chosen as St. Cecilia's, is indeed fortunate. In so far, such parish is working inestimable good toward Church and State.

ST. CECILIA'S MATERNITY HOSPITAL.

Before giving an account of the establishment and work of St. Cecilia Maternity Hospital, it is most fitting to insert copy of a sermon delivered by Father McGolrick from the pulpit of St. James' Pro-Cathedral, January 23rd, 1902, over the remains of Brooklyn's heroic, successful, Catholic Obstetrician and General Practitioner, the eminent Dr. Dominic G. Bodkin.

While such sermon grandly places the Doctor's name and fame in memoriam; while it contributes to this book type of the pastor's scholarly eloquence; while it enlightens the many, through Doctor Bodkin's life, on the thoroughness and culture of Irish education; yet, not for any or all of these reasons is it reprinted here. It is set down on this occasion because in it we find stressed the conscientious obligation ruling child-birth which sacred duty was never forgotten or ignored by the great Dr. Bodkin. And it is this very emphasis of the physician's duty which seems now to have been the preacher's foreshadowing of the conscientious work which was to be carried out within the then unthought-of St. Cecilia Maternity Hospital.

THE LATE DOMINICK G. BODKIN, M. D.

Impressive Service Over the Remains of Brooklyn's Most Emi-
nent Physician.—Rev. Edward J. McGolrick's Well-
Merited Tribute.—At St. James' Pro-Cathedral,
Brooklyn, Thursday, January 23, 1902.

I have fought a good fight, I have finished my course, I have kept
the faith. For the rest there is laid up for me a crown of justice, which
the Lord, the just judge, will render to me at that day—II. Ep. St. Paul
to Timothy, iv. 7.

Rt. Rev. Bishop, Very Rev. and Rev. Fathers,
Beloved Brethren:

We are assembled here this morning to pay the last tribute
of respect to one whom we all loved and honored in life. We
loved him for for his many lovable and admirable qualities,
and we honored him because of his magnificent personality.

Within that casket there lie two feet that never wearied of
responding to the call of duty. There, too, clasped in death's
embrace, repose two hands that have performed countless acts
of kindness—hands that in life were so gentle yet strong, whose
touch seemed to assuage pain, and whose firm grasp made us
feel we were in presence of a man. That tongue, whose well
modulated accents so oft brought consolation, encouragement,
hope to many a dejected heart, and which was such a source
of joy in his own household, will speak no more. Within that
casket forever stilled there is a heart that beat with loving
sympathy for suffering humanity, whether the sufferer was the
child just born or the centenarian tottering toward the grave;
whether it was the depraved outcast, or a venerable servant of
God; whether it was the poor beggar by the wayside or the

wealthy aristocrat surrounded by all the luxuries that money could procure, for one and all that great heart throbbed with a sympathetic chord.

"Dr. Bodkin is dead." When the announcement was made a few days ago in the daily papers many citizens of this Borough of Brooklyn felt that they had lost one of their dearest friends, aye, one of their household, for is not the doctor in a most particular manner a member of the home into which his ministrations call him. The doctor is mourned to-day in many homes with a sorrow just a little less keen than would be the sorrow for a member of the family.

A short review of his life will be no less interesting than edifying.

The doctor was born near Galway, Ireland, in the year 1833. He comes of one of the most distinguished families in the western part of Ireland. The Bodkins and the Bourkes or de Burgos are names found in connection with every effort made by our forefathers for God or their native land. The Bodkins were recognized leaders among their countrymen.

His Uncle the First Bishop of Galway Since the Reformation.

The doctor's first preceptor was his distinguished uncle Bishop O'Donnell, then Bishop of Galway (the first bishop since the Reformation), under whom he studied until his 14th year. This fact may no doubt answer the question many of you have so often asked: How comes it that Dr. Bodkin had such a mastery over the English language? How comes it that this man whom we considered self-educated, who claimed no preparatory college as his Alma Mater should manifest from time to time such an intimate knowledge with the classics? It was within the last few weeks I learned what I now narrate. Standing by his bedside one morning I remarked the wonderful depth and clearness of his voice and said, "Doctor, that voice gives no indication of weakness." His answer was: "Vox et præterea nihil." This little phrase so appropriately uttered caused us to speak of the classics, and then it was that he told me that at the age of 6 he began the study of Greek and Latin under his uncle, the Bishop of Galway, and who had been his teacher until his 14th year. He told me, moreover, that few years passed since during which he did not translate one of the Greek authors.

His Parents Died on Landing in America.

When the deceased reached his 14th year the family came to this country. A few weeks after their arrival a malignant fever carried off both parents. Relatives in Ireland sent for the children, and all returned to their native land, but the eldest son, Dominic, whose remains lie here this morning. He, an orphan of 14, courageously resolved to stay in New York, though friendless and almost penniless, and carve out a pathway for himself. How well he succeeded this large and representative audience gives but eloquent testimony.

When the rebellion broke out the orphan boy had grown to manhood, and we found him near the cherished goal of his ambition. He had by dint of brawn and brain and magnificent will power reached the graduating class of the New York University Medical College. In a few months he would have been in possession of his diploma.

Like a thunderbolt from a clear sky comes the awful news that Fort Sumpter had been fired upon, the South had seceded, the Union was in danger—the call for volunteers. This news stirred every fiber in every true man's heart, and found no more responsive nor generous answer anywhere than in the great Celtic heart of Dominic Bodkin.

Enters the Army.

Personal ambition is cast aside; he gives up all for his adopted country, enters the army and is assigned to the ambulance corps. Not having his degrees, he ranked as a nurse. In short while his worth is appreciated and he is acting as physician and surgeon. He remained in the army until the cause for which he sacrificed so much had triumphed and then modestly returned to continue his studies. He received his degrees from the New York University Medical College in the year 1866.

Since that time his career has been an open book; on every page of which may be discerned, not with the eye of the body, but with the eye of the spirit, the most beautiful illuminations. The subject matter is there glowing with life and pathos, and needs but the soul of an artist to bring it forth to life and light. Who was ever more devoted to duty?

Multitudes Continually Sought His Aid.

What doctor of the present day or generation had such a practice? He was a general practitioner, yet in one branch, obstetrics, his annual returns to the Health Board was for eight or ten years more than 1,000 cases each year. Never did he refuse his services when called on, no matter how great the distance, how cold the night or warm the day, or poor the patient. He was, of a truth, a Napoleon in the practice of medicine, knowing no distraction by day or night and sleeping only when forced to do so; often in his carriage, in going from one call to another.

Delegate to Foreign Medical Conventions.

During these years his only vacations were practically forced upon him when he was sent abroad by his brother physicians to represent them at the medical conventions of London, Paris, Berlin and St. Petersburg.

I could not, if I wanted to, narrate the one-hundredth part of the heroic acts of this busy life. Most of them were performed where none but the all-seeing eye of God and the Recording Angel could witness them. For far less heroism than he has exhibited, not on one, but on 10,000 occasions, men have been the recipients of the button of the Legion of Honor, the Victoria Cross, or some equally prized decoration. Reward sufficient for him was to feel the sweet consciousness of having performed his duty and of obtaining a place in the affections of his fellow creatures.

His Career in Obstetrics.

In obstetrics his career will be spoken of in years to come as fabulous and inconceivable. In the eyes of the physicians of the future his life will appear as extraordinary, as does the life of a saint to the ordinary Christian.

In obstetrics he has left an impression not surpassed in results by Poird, Leopold, Sager, Murdock, Cameron, Sir Dominick Corrigan or a Lusk. His successes were more wonderful than his calls. His success was owing, we believe, to these three reasons:

First—Because of the awful consciousness of the tremendous responsibility of the doctor.

Second—He realized the dignity of the human soul created by God and destined for immortality. He knew well he had no rights over the soul; that one life was as precious as another; that the un-Christian principle that the end justifies the means never found a habitation in his mind.

Third—His duty was to assist, to aid, to wait, not to destroy

We feel certain that if our dear deceased friend could speak this morning he would repeat with more vehemence than I can and declare as his own the sentiments uttered by Dr. James Murphy, president of the British Medical Association in his address before that society on the occasion of its annual meeting in the year 1893:

"I say it deliberately, and with whatever authority I possess—and I urge it with all the force I can master—that we are not justified in destroying a living child; and while there may be some things I look back upon with pleasure in my professional career, that which gives me the greatest satisfaction is that I have never done a craniotomy on a living child."

A Profound Scholar as Well as a Great Physician.

Besides being a great physician, we recognize in the doctor a ripe and profound scholar, a charming conversationalist, and an orator of wonderful ability, and a linguist. He spoke Irish, French and German, and was conversant with Greek and Latin, as we have already intimated. He was a credit to his race and a shining light in his profession; and in his private life he was the joy and admiration of all those who had the good fortune to be numbered among his friends.

Never were the words of Shakespeare more aptly applied than to Dr. Dominick Bodkin:

> Where every god did seem to set his seal,
>
> A combination, and a form, indeed,
>
> To give the world assurance of a man.

As a child of the Church, what shall we say of him? Here the words of my text are most eminently fitting: "I have fought a good fight; I have finished my course; I have kept the faith." If the great Apostle of the Gentiles could compliment himself on the fact that he had kept the faith, truly and justly may we compliment our dear deceased friend in doing like-wise; and equally can we hope that the Lord, the just judge has rendered or will soon render unto him that crown, the reward of faith and charity.

The Time That Tried Men's Souls.

When we consider the surroundings of this life just brought to a close, we have to stand in admiration at the great and glorious fight he has fought. Think of that bright and ambitious Irish boy of fourteen in New York some fifty years ago, when both our race and creed were despised and ridiculed; when every avenue to preferment was closed; when the only obstacle to obtain even an inferior position was the misfortune

of being Irish; when those advertising for help boldly an-
nounced "No Irish need apply." Under such circumstances
sorry we are to say, some denied their religion—aye, even
some of his companions—but with him opposition only strength-
ened his faith. Did his career in the medical school tend to a
fostering of the spirit of religion? With all due respect for the
medical profession and to the many great and good Christian
men therein, that profession which runs on parallel lines with
the priesthood itself, and which may, in a certain sense, apply
to itself the words of St. Paul: "Sumus einem Dei adjutores."
(We are the coadjutors of God in corporal matters as the
priests are in spiritual matters). Such being the case, I assert
the medical schools of forty years ago were not, as they are
not to-day, seminaries of spirituality; on the contrary, we find
therein a strong spirit of materialism and agnosticism. From
such a school the doctor came forth unscathed.

What will you say of the army, where he spent four years?
Do we not know of many young men leaving Christian homes
coming back from the army with depraved morals and blighted
faith? Hence, well might the deceased say: "I have fought a
good fight—I have kept the faith." During the many years of
his most engrossing medical practice he was not able to attend
to the outward practices of our holy faith as his Christian
heart would wish; but, despite this, faith chilled not, as was
most evident when he felt the end drawing near. Like the
humblest child of the Church, he calls to his bedside the priest
of God, and that priest one whom he had attended in boyhood, youth and manhood. He forgets the man and considers
but the ambassador of Christ. Fortified by the Sacraments, he
calmly and resignedly and with great Christian fortitude awaits
the end. Never did we see a more patient sufferer. Never did
any one await the final summons with such dignity and hero-

ism; to the last moment fully conscious, thoughtful of others and grateful for every little kindness.

In his passing away I was forcibly reminded of a monument I saw a few years ago in the Church of St. Thomas in the city of Strasbourg, erected to the memory of Prince Conde, the great military leader of the sixteenth century. On the face of the monument we see the prince dressed in the uniform of the marshal, with epaulets, sword and spurs, in the act of descending a flight of stairs; at the bottom there is an open tomb, and sitting on the side of the tomb is Death beckoning the marshal to come on. This was entirely ideal, the conception of the sculptor. We can say that in the death of Dr. Bodkin we saw the reality; courage without presumption, resignation unalloyed with despair.

In opening my discourse I said we came here to honor the deceased. We are assembled here for a still higher and holier purpose; we have come here to pray for the soul of our departed friend. In keeping with the teaching of the inspired writings, and of holy mother church, and in accordance with the tradition of 2,000 years, we believe that "it is a holy and wholesome thought to pray for the dead," that they may be loosed from their sins. Hence, in his name, I ask you to pray for him. No matter how Christian and praiseworthy our lives may be, we are at our best most imperfect. How can that which is imperfect expect to be worthy of immediate admittance into Heaven, to join the angelic choir where the angels veil their faces in the presence of God? We are, then, consoled and comforted by the thought of a middle state, where some souls are detained for a time, that they may be cleansed and purified from the scars of sin from the imperfections belonging to us who have been conceived in sin. 'Twas the thought of purgatory helped the deceased to bear so heroically with his great sufferings.

He said to himself and to others: "It is evident that God wishes me to suffer; better, therefore, suffer here than hereafter. Thy will be done, O Lord!"

As you have loved him in life, I now ask you to pray for him dead. Harken to his call: "Have pity on me; at least you, my friends."

Now, dear doctor and friend, in the name of the thousands of children whom you ushered into life, some of whom without your skill might never have been washed in the regenerating waters of baptism, some of whom are here in the church, representatives of every walk of life, aye, even of the priesthood, medicine and law, I say in their name, "Thanks and farewell!" In the name of the poor, who have lost a dear friend and benefactor, "Thanks and farewell!" In the name of all those whom you have assisted by your medical skill, "Thanks and farewell!" In the name of your brother physicians, who ever looked up to you as a model of all that was best, noblest and most honorable. "Thanks and farewell!" In the name of the bereaved family, the tenderest chords of whose hearts vibrated with purest love for their dear departed, and who looked up to him as does the mariner toward the polar star, I say "Farewell, brother; farewell, uncle!"

In the name of our Right Rev. Bishop and priests here present, and of this vast congregation, because of the good fight you have fought and to the example given, "Thanks and farewell!"

In the name of all, and from the bottom of our hearts we say: "Eternal rest grant to him, O Lord, and let perpetual light shine upon him!"

"May his soul and the souls of the faithful departed, rest in peace."

FINDING WORTHY USE FOR THE "SETTLEMENT HOUSE."

The parish had immediate use for only one of the two buildings purchased from the Brooklyn Industrial School Society in 1922. The larger building known hitherto as the "Settlement House" was offered to the Bishop as a Diocesan High School. The Bishop accepted the offer with many thanks, but in another year found he was not able to put it to the use intended.

At this time a few articles in different magazines fell to the Pastor's notice. One article was entitled, "The High Cost of Babies," another equally forceful and impressive was captioned, "What Cost Baby."

It was then the thought arose of establishing a Maternity Hospital where charity work might go hand in hand with paid work. Many physicians and a few clergymen were consulted. All agreed, that there was need of such an institution. The Bishop was then consulted and was in hearty accord, giving generous help to finance the project.

The "Settlement Building" was greatly enlarged and the entire interior re-arranged to suit Hospital requirements. The full cost amounting to two hundred fifteen thousand dollars. The people of the vicinity, irrespective of creed or politics, gave generous assistance. Today there rests upon the Hospital an indebtedness of only about twenty thousand dollars.

Solemn Blessing of St. Cecilia Maternity Hospital.

On Sunday, January sixteenth, nineteen hundred twenty seven, the Right Reverend Thomas E. Molloy, D. D., Bishop of Brooklyn, solemnly blessed the St. Cecilia Maternity Hospital.

RT. REV. THOMAS E. MOLLOY, D. D.

Third Bishop of Brooklyn

SOUVENIR BOOKLET.

The Booklet commemorative of the event contains a photographic likeness of the Right Reverend Bishop Molloy, D. D., of the Founder of the hospital, the Rt. Rev. Monsignor McGolrick, LL. D., and of a liberal and distinguished benefactor, the Right Reverend Thomas J. Shahan, D. D., J. U. D., then Rector of the Catholic University of America, Washington, D. C.

It tells what Sisters are in charge of the institution and gives a brief description of their Convent home "hidden away in a corner of the building." There is also an interesting article written by the Founder on "The Catholic Church and Hospital."

On the following pages the contents of this Souvenir Booklet are reprinted in their entirety.

RT. REV. THOMAS J. SHAHAN, D. D., J. U. D.

Rector of Catholic University, Washington, D. C.

THE SISTERS OF ST. DOMINIC IN CHARGE OF ST. CECILIA MATERNITY HOSPITAL.

(From Souvenir Booklet)

"The Maternity Hospital of the Greenpoint section of our great city of New York throws its doors open today for the reception of patients, amid the rejoicing of the people of this district, the solemn blessing of Holy Mother Church and, we firmly trust, with the benediction of Heaven on this long needed House of Mercy.

"In one section of the Hospital there is quietly hidden away a Dominican Convent with its kitchen, reception room, dormitory and its tasteful chapel. In the chapel there self-sacrificing daughters of St. Dominic will find inspiration, comfort and joy beyond expression since they may there commune with Christ the Lord dwelling in the Tabernacle and consider their life of sacrifice and insignificant in comparison with all that Christ has done for and promises to those who love Him.

These daughters of St. Dominic, specially trained in hospital work, will be in charge to look after the proper management of every department of the institution and to meet you with a smile whether you come as patient or friend of patient."

THE CATHOLIC CHURCH AND HOSPITAL.

Monsignor McGolrick

(Reprinted from Souvenir Booklet)

'Tis with feelings of gladness, not un-alloyed with pride, that the pastor and people of St. Cecilia's bid you welcome here today on this the occasion of the solemn blessing of our St. Cecilia Maternity.

Gladness fills our hearts to behold another building added to our already quite numerous parochial buildings, and rivaling in architectural beauty those already erected to the glory of God, and the spiritual, intellectual and corporal welfare of our fellow man. Joy fills our hearts, too, because, on these great monuments of the vitality of our Holy Church, there is very little indebtedness; insignificant in comparison to the value of our property. This Maternity as it stands today, means an expenditure of over Two Hundred Thousand Dollars ($200,000.00) and on our entire holdings we have less than Twenty-five Thousand Dollars ($25,000.00) indebtedness.

Pride likewise occupies a very prominent place in our hearts today; we consider, however, that it is a laudable pride. The inspired writer says: "So let your light shine before men, that they may see your good works and glorify your Father who is in heaven." Matt. 5-16. We are proud of the extraordinary accomplishment of the loyal and devoted people of St. Cecilia's parish. With little or no superabundance of worldly goods, nay the vast majority struggling for their daily sustenance, parochial buildings have been erected by them that are not surpassed in stability or architectural beauty by any parish in this great country. Today the principal reason for our joy and pride is the Maternity Hospital with all the latest and most approved appointments that can be found in such an institution, and with a capacity for sixty-five patients, with accommodations for the Sisters of St. Dominic, nurses and doctors. This Maternity, though erected by the people of St. Cecilia's parish, will not be parochial in its work of caring for the prospective mothers; all will be received irrespective of race or creed. We wish to state that people of many races and creeds, Jews and Gentiles, have helped us in the erection of this hospice of mercy.

What induced us to undertake this work? From the encominums we have received on all sides, from the forceful and practical approbation given by our Rt. Rev. Bishop Thos. E. Molloy, from the princely donations received from some we have never seen and from some not of the fold, we flatter ourselves with what may be a most presumptuous thought that God willed this hospital should be erected in this vicinity. The physical as well as the spiritual well-being of poor weak human nature have ever been closely allied in the mind of Christ's Church, just as they were allied in the mind and heart of Christ Himself.

The physical well being of man was dear to the heart of our Divine Lord. Body and soul are most intimately united forming one person; the body is the tabernacle, in which dwells an immortal soul made to the image of God and destined to live throughout an endless eternity. Through and by the body, the soul is cleansed from sin, is united to Christ in the Holy Eucharist, is sanctified by the Holy Ghost. Therefore the body is something just a little less sacred than the soul, and it too is destined for life eternal, therefore it is that in the sight of the Church of God the body is treated with such consideration and distinction.

Christ began His public career by that sublime and truly divine sermon on the Mount, which filled His hearers with profound admiration since they realized He was teaching them as one having power and not as their Scribes and Pharisees.

As He came down from the mountain, the multitude still following Him, behold a leper came and adored Him, saying: "Lord, if Thou wilt, Thou canst make me clean." And Jesus, stretching forth His hand, touched him, saying, "I will, be thou made clean," and forewith his leprosy was cleansed. Soon after this, entering into Capharnum a Centurion came to Him and said, "Lord, my servant lieth at home sick of the palsy and is grievously tormented." Jesus said to him, "I will come and heal him," and the Centurion said, "I am not worthy that Thou shouldst enter under my roof, but only say the word and my servant shall be healed." And Jesus said to the Centurion: "Go and as thou hast believed, so be it done to thee." And the servant was healed at that same hour. On this first journey after the sermon on the Mount, He arrived at Peter's house and found Peter's wife's mother sick of a fever. He touched her hand and the fever left her, and she arose and ministered unto them. When the evening of that day was come they brought to Him many that were possessed with devils and He cast out the spirits with His words and all that were sick He healed. Truly and justly therefore may Christ the King be called, "Christ the greatest of physicians."

Of the seven Sacraments instituted by our Divine Lord, one was instituted as a source of comfort and relief to the debilitated body.

Extreme Unction—In the words of St. James, we are told, "Is any one sick among you, let him bring in the priest of the Church, let him pray over him, anointing him with oil, and the prayer of faith shall save the sick man."

St. Peter began his apostolic work by curing the man who sat begging near the door of the temple. This man had been lame from his mother's womb, and was carried there each day. As Peter passed by he asked for an alms. Peter said to him, "Silver or gold I have none, but what I have I give thee, in the name of the Lord Jesus Christ of Nazareth, arise and walk," and the lame man was cured of his infirmity.

Acts, Chap. 3 VI.

From the earliest days of Christianity there was a well organized system of providing for the various forms of suffering. When the Emperor Julian the apostate arose against the Christ—that was but fifty years after the Christians were permitted the free exercise of their religion—one of his means of combat was to erect a hospital in every city and town in the East where the Christians had hospitals; this we learn in letter Julian wrote to Arsacius, high-priest of Galatia. Julian plainly declared that his motive was to rival the philanthropic work of the Christians who cared for the pagans as well as for their own. During the plague in Edessa in the year 375, St. Ephraem provided three hundred beds for the plague stricken. The most famous of the early Christian hospitals was in Caeserea, in Capadocia, known as the "Basilia," which had the dimensions of a city with its regular streets, its buildings for different classes of patients, dwellings for nurses and physicians, workshops and trade schools. St. Gregory of Nazianzus writes in the most commendatory manner of this wonderful institution which he calls an easy ascent to heaven. The earliest hospital foundation of Rome of which we have any record was in the year 400 when Fabiola established a hospital to gather in the sick from the streets and to nurse the wretched sufferers wasted with poverty and disease. 'Tis from St. Chrysostom, Doctor of the Church, that we learn this in his epistle on the death of Fabiola.

As Christianity spread in Europe, so did hospitals. When the Irish monks came down through Belgium, France, Switzerland and Italy, evangelizing the natives, they likewise built monasteries and hospitals. We learn this from the National Council of Meaux held in the year 845, nearly eleven hundred years ago. At this council, the Bishops ordered the restoration of the hospitals of the Irish monks. Between the 11th and 15th centuries in the city of Rome, thirty hospitals were erected.

One of the most wonderful hospitals in the world today by reason of its size, its adaptability to the purposes for which it was erected, and by reason of the numbers of patients it can shelter, containing usually more than 2,000 patients, is the Grand Hospital of Milan, erected in the year 1456, which

means 36 years before America was discovered and 54 years
before Luther rebelled against the Church. This hospital, as a
non-Catholic writer tells us, is a good example of what has
been attained towards the development of hospitals and shows
how much a part of the Church the institution of hospitals is.

Our great medical schools are the outgrowth of hospitals.
The schools of Salerno, Naples, Bologna, Paris, began in hospitals. The Church has religious orders of men and women
dedicated to almost every phase of bodily suffering from
foundling asylums to homes for the aged.—E. J. McGolrick.

MONSIGNOR McGOLRICK REALIZES
DREAM AS HOSPITAL FLOURISHES.

Brooklyn Daily Times, December 1, 1929.

St. Cecilia Maternity Institution Has Recorded But One Death
of Over 1700 Treated In Three Years.

The night of November 9, 1888, was momentous in the history of Greenpoint, for then, in the midst of a black rain, a
young man swung from a street car and plodded up Herbert
Street. It was the new priest, Father Edward J. McGolrick,
come to take charge of the struggling parish of St. Cecilia's.

Now, 41 years after, he is the Rt. Rev. Monsignor McGolrick and the parish is known for its prosperity and works the
country over. Within its square block of parochial property
are provisions for the welfare of mind, body and soul of its
people from birth to death.

There is the church, a Romanesque pile rising in the beauty
and majesty of marble and granite; the Rt. Rev. John Loughlin Memorial Lyceum, seating 600, and housing stage, billiard

and card rooms, and swimming pool; the monastery for the Christian Brothers; the convent for the Sisters of St. Joseph; the great school building; the library; the priests' house and the Maternity Hospital.

Had Small Beginning.

All those spring from the little clap-board church, now preserved in the Lyceum building. The growth was slow. The young priest came to a parish burdened by debt and dissension. He entered the pulpit and went among the people with the one desire, only to bring them the teaching of the church. Other matters did not exist for him except as secondary. Greenpoint saw he was sincere and flocked to him.

Perhaps the greatest minute in all those years came in the first. Attendance at St. Cecilia's had been dropping away not only because of a number of unfortunate events, but partly because of a purely physical discomfort. The roof leaked. The new priest staved off the creditors, skimped and saved, and at last was able to pay for a pine ceiling.

His eyes glinted with the memory of the minute when the first hammers thudded upon the nail heads as he talked of that time today.

"I shall never forget the joy that came to me then," he said. "It was the first tangible step forward."

And so, little by little, success came. The priest took opportunities as they presented themselves, took them in such a way that other opportunities grew from them.

Such an opportunity formed the beginning of St. Cecilia's Maternity Hospital, dedicated January 16, 1927, and opened the following February 2 to the women of the city, the first Roman Catholic institution of its kind in the country.

Parish Needed Building.

The parish had needed a building for a day nursery, and Mons. McGolrick had thought of the buildings of the J. W. Smith Memorial, then almost in disuse. In characteristically straightforward fashion, he went to the attorney for the trustees. He asked a ridiculously low figure, but a little more than the parish was conveniently ready to pay. Mons. McGolrick offered $5,000 less. It was accepted.

But only one building was needed for the nursery, and the other, he felt, should not be left idle. Mons. McGolrick cast about in his mind and thought of the needs of his people. He recalled how often the birth of a child, because of the mounting expense, had been made an event of sadness, when it should have been one of joy. He sought Divine guidance. Then he decided upon the radical step.

The Rt. Rev. Bishop Thomas E. Molloy gave the project his sanction and financial assistance.

From loyal friends and the 11,000 parishioners, came the funds. The building was remodeled and extended at a cost of more than $215,000. Nothing was spared to make the hospital modern in every detail, from the receiving rooms to the wards.

At the time of the dedication, a Brooklyn Times reporter inspected the building and was impressed with the brightness of the rooms, all of which have at least two windows opening onto unobstructed sunshine, the spic-and-span operating rooms, the diet kitchens, the automatic elevators, the electric refrigerators, the electric apparatus for heating the babies' blankets, the appliances of every kind best adapted to the care of the patients.

But today, with all these facilities in actual use, the fact proved better than the promise. Since the opening there have been approximately 1,700 women enter the hospital and but one was lost, a record hardly to be equalled in any other similar institution and nowhere approached by the average of maternity cases treated at home.

Not all the 40 ward beds were occupied nor all the 16 private rooms. It so happened that many mothers, purely by coincidence, had been discharged on the eve of Thanksgiving day.

But some were still waiting for the 11th day to come, the day on which they may be allowed to go home. Ministering to them were the nine registered nurses and the four Sisters of St. Dominic who have charge of the hospital.

Not one of the mothers was there who did not smile when the visitors, Mons. McGolrick, Sister Mercedes, and the reporter paused.

Roman Catholic, Jew, Protestant, agnostic—all are sisters in the sight of St. Cecilia, and are admitted to her house for equal care. Only the flutter of the sisters' robes, the crucifix on the wall of the ward, the statues of the Saint and the Virgin in the corridors remind one the hospital is a religious foundation.

Forty Staff Physicians.

On its staff are 40 of the leading physicians, surgeons and specialists of the city. One's own family doctor may work there. And rich and poor may have the best care science and tenderness can give.

ST. CECILIA HOSPITAL FOR WOMEN.

Very recently, the name of the Maternity Hospital was changed to "St. Cecilia Hospital for Women." This was done in answer to many and insistent requests to admit women for other than maternity cases.

The Hospital is approved by the New York State Board of Hospitals and by the American College of Surgeons.

ST. CECILIA HOSPITAL FOR WOMEN

STATEMENT OF MONEY CONTRIBUTED BY THE PEOPLE OF
ST. CECILIA PARISH

For our New Diocesan Seminary at Huntington, L. I.

NOVEMBER 1929

In the name of our Right Reverend Bishop Thomas E. Molloy, D. D., we thank all those who have contributed to this collection. Our quota was $20,000.00. We have thus far collected $14,069.62.

Monsignor McGolrick, Pastor
Rev. James H. A. Dolan
Rev. Edmund J. Carey
Rev. Eugene McLoughlin.

Miscellaneous

Monsignor McGolrick	$600.00
Rev. Jas. H. A. Dolan	50.00
Rev. Edmund Carey	50.00
Rev. Eugene McLoughlin	50.00
Boys of St. Cecilia School	416.31
St. Aloysius Sodality	75.00
Alumnae Society	100.00
Girls of Our School	56.31
Mr. Max Trunz	150.00
In Memory of J. P. Clark	25.00
Mr. Robert A. Caufield	25.00
Mr. Cavagnaro	20.00
Mr. and Mrs. Luritzen	20.00
Anonymous	17.00
In Memory of J. Schneller	10.00
Wm. Healy (Calyer St.)	20.00
J. Downey (O. W. Road)	17.00
Miss McMahon	10.00
Edward Flynn Family	10.00
In Memory of	
Mrs. Mary Olmstead	10.00
Mr. & Mrs. F.E.Lammers	10.00
Mr. & Mrs. Raym. Oldis	10.00

Charles McDonough	5.00
A. M. D. G.	5.00
Miss A. Solan	5.00
Mr. Reardon	5.00
Raym. & Gertrude Oldis	5.00
Mrs. Elizabeth Skehan	10.00
Miss Jennie Skehan	5.00

Apollo Street

Mr. John Cox	$16.00
James Watson	5.00
Harry Wareing	10.00
William Hefferan	20.00
Edward McCauley	2.00
John Farley	1.00
William Keeler	5.00
In Memory of	
Dora Sheppard	5.00
William Owens	5.00
In Memory of	
Mrs. Margaret Owens	5.00
James Owens	5.00
Margaret Owens	2.00
Anna Owens	2.00

Apollo Street

Francis J. Canavan	20.00
James McGrattan	5.00
Thomas McGrattan	2.00
Ann McGrattan	1.00
Raymond Hall	2.00
James J. Gibney	15.00
E. Clark	5.00
Mrs. Ellen Finnegan	25.00
Patrick McKenna	10.00
Mrs. Nellie McCartney	3.00
Mr. & Mrs. P. Timmons	17.00
Patrick Lydon	3.00
In Memory of	
James Conway	10.00
Thomas Schlitz	25.00
John O'Connor	5.00
Joseph Alexander	2.00
Sarah McCauley	3.00
Thomas Carson, Sr.	5.00
Thomas Carson, Jr.	5.00
James Muldoon & Family	10.00
John Rodonski	5.00
Arthur Reynolds	25.00
In Memory of	
John and Mary Nelson	40.00
Joseph McEvoy	3.00
Mr. & Mrs. Michael Boyle	30.00
William Boyle	20.00
William J. Gillen	30.00
William Connors	5.00
Charles Vorbach	3.00
Henry Ladewig	3.00
Patrick Stanton	7.00
Mary Stanton	1.00
Catherine Stanton	1.00
John Stanton	1.00
Fred. J. Haupert	15.00
Richard Doherty	7.00
Frances Salutt	2.00

Apollo Street

Mrs. Ann Foley	20.00
Mrs. Margaret Dempsey	10.00
Mrs. William Huber	5.00
Mrs. Edward King	3.00
In Memory of	
William Flannagan	
and James Seymour	5.00
John T. Conway	20.00

Beadel Street

Martin Hublitz	$1.00
Patrick Moran	10.00
Bernard McLaughlin	5.00
William Gordan	3.00
Mary Gordan	2.00
John Mills	5.00
Adam Clifford	2.00
Mrs. Julia Ackerly	15.00
Deak Family	50.00
Miss Marion Stravorsky	10.00
C. McAllister	10.00
James McAllister	2.00
James Clancy	5.00
Arthur Quinn	2.00
Herman Lenninger	2.00
Lawrence Brown	5.00
John Marron	2.00
William Pritchard	5.00
E. Burkett	5.00
In Memory of	
John Stockman	2.00
Mr. & Mrs. B. Stockman	8.00
Ed. Reilly	2.00
Thomas Foye	3.00
Mrs. Reiser	2.00
Bernard Reiser	3.00
John Graaf	1.00
Mary Graaf	1.00
Mr. and Mrs. P. Coyne	10.00
Wm. Jewell and Family	5.00

Beadel Street

John Armstrong	3.00
In Memory of	
William Tooker	5.00
Mrs. F. Tooker	5.00
John Reardon	6.00
Deah Family	50.00
Mr. Stamsky	10.00
George Hillary	10.00
Francis Garlan	2.00

Broome Street

Mr. Michael Kelly and	
Family	$20.00
Thomas J. Kelly	35.00
James O'Gara	5.00
In Memory of	
Mary F. Malone	2.00
Hugh A. Reid	2.00
Mr. & Mrs. Wm. L. Hayes	22.00

Diamond Street

Mrs. E. Gaffney	$2.00
Hugh Gilroy	30.00
In Memory of	
Patk. and Bryan Gilroy	20.00
William Hines	2.00
Mrs. Schwartz	2.00
Walter J. Brennan	1.00
Laurence Nugent	5.00
George Dubois	3.00
Stephen Donovan	15.00
William Crowley	25.00
Robert Mallgraf	2.00
Mrs. Becker	2.00
George Reilly	5.00
Mary Reilly	5.00
Mrs. Sarah Parker	5.00
Margaret Mullins	5.00
Anna Kelly	3.00
William McKenna	3.00
Joseph Kesler	5.00

Driggs Avenue

Martin Molloy	$20.00
In Memory of	
William Nicholson	5.00
Adam Nicolaus	10.00
John F. McAlister	2.00
Mrs. Teresa McAlister	1.00
Anna McAlister	1.00
William Mitchell	5.00
Adolph Schneider	1.00
James Rossiter	1.00
George Schwally	5.00
Fred. Schwally	2.00
Mrs. George Schwally	3.00
John Rohan	3.00
Patrick Fee	5.00
James Tunny	5.00
Edward Plunkett	3.00
Mrs. Anna Plunkett	7.00
Marie Plunkett	3.00
James Plunkett	1.00
Samuel Kelly	3.00
Julius Graff	2.00
Patrick Gerrity	5.00
Fred. Lamneck	3.00
Anthony Lally	3.00
John Brett	3.00
John Huether	1.00
Anthony Guidice	1.00
In Memory of	
Mrs. Weber	15.00
William Durr	3.00
James Maher	5.00
George Hopf	7.00
William Tholl	3.00
Andrew Boyle	5.00
Patrick McGrattan	5.00
Thomas Stickley	23.00
John Hern	60.00
Mr. & Mrs. Peter Hearn	5.00

Driggs Avenue

Cormac Hearn	10.00
Cecilia Hearn	3.00
Matilda Hearn	5.00
Florence Hearn	1.00
William Greene	4.00
John McDonough	2.00
Charles McAvoy	2.00
Joseph Volpone	15.00
Anna Volpone	2.00
Mrs. M. Canning	10.00
Bartholomew Basso	15.00
Andrew J. Cavagnaro	5.00
Patrick J. Corbett	5.00
Joseph Corbett	1.00
Eddie Corbett	1.00
Catherine Corbett	1.00
Nora Corbett	1.00
Harry Keifner. Sr.	2.00
Harry Keifner	1.00
George Reid	5.00
Mrs. Henry Hopf	5.00
Mrs. Anna Mullins	5.00
Mrs. Margaret Stickley	22.00
Michael O'Connor	5.00
Charles N. Fletcher	5.00
Mrs. Susan Walsh	2.00
Charles Dorman	2.00
Mrs. A. Decker	15.00
Mrs. Cusack	20.00
Mrs. J. Donlon & Family	40.00
Margaret Logan	5.00
Mrs. Kennedy	3.00
Michael Walsh	5.00
Mrs. McGuire	1.00
Elizabeth McGuire	1.00
John McGuire	1.00
Anna Canning	2.00

Eckford Street

Michael Neary	$2.00

Eckford Street

Miss Tierney	2.00
Catherine Savery	2.00
John Holland	20.00
Mrs. Jas. Grant & Family	5.00
Michael Devaney	5.00

Engert Avenue

Mrs. Josephine Donges	$5.00
Henry Blickhahn	1.00
Frank Munsterman	2.00
Mrs. Peter J. Stenger	5.00
John Slowey	5.00
Sophie Herb	2.00
John Galligan	5.00
William Whearty	3.00
Mrs. Kenny	5.00
Neil McLoughlin	3.00
Martin Brennen	2.00
Zenon Closawicz	1.00
John Gyves	5.00
William Plant	45.00
Catherine Plant	5.00
George Young	2.00
Robert Tucker	2.00
Peter Dwyer	5.00
William Knapp	3.00
Francis McEnaney	2.00
Mrs. Neil and Family	5.00
John Hickey	5.00
John Stevens and Family	5.00
James Kearney	2.00
James Cahalan	3.00
John McClosky	3.00
Christine Brady	1.00
Frank Brady	1.00
In Memory of	
Edward and Edna Meyer	5.00
Anna Walsh	5.00
Ellen Hushen	23.00
John Hushen	22.00

Engert Avenue

George Stiesi	3.00
Peter J. Adams	2.00
Mrs. Mary E. Cassidy	2.00
W. J. Carroll	3.00
Patrick McGee	5.00
Mr. and Mrs. Andrew Fitzpatrick	4.00
Grace Smith	2.00
In Memory of Edward and Ann Caulfield	20.00
Catherine Ward	2.00
Mrs. C. & Miss V. Lenhart	10.00
James McCabe	30.00
John McCabe	2.00
Loretta McCabe	1.00
Mrs. Helen Connaughton	3.00
Mrs. R. L. McFarland	5.00
Mrs. W. H. Browne	8.00
Miss Agnes Collins	2.00
May Caulfield	10.00
Thomas & Mary Gardiner	20.00

Frost Street

Matthew Dugan	$5.00
Richard Dugan	5.00
Denis Kelleher	5.00
Frank Kraemer	5.00
Mr. Timmons	$5.00

Graham Avenue

In Memory of Mrs. Ellen Cumberland	$2.00
Mary and Elizabeth McDonough	2.00
Jeanie Keenan	1.00
Peter J. Maguire	2.00
Mr. and Mrs. Russo	1.00
Mrs. Mendola	1.00
Vito Tota	1.00
Mrs. Moody & Mrs. Ramsey	2.00
Jos. and Mrs. Rhaner	3.00

Graham Avenue

J. P. Clark & Co.	20.00
John and Mrs. Smith	3.00
M. Esposito	1.00
Charles Cooke	10.00
Michael Pellegrini	1.00
Mrs. Catherine Strohm	5.00
August Sounsen	10.00
Eugene Price	5.00
Charles Uhlinger & Son	10.00
Mrs. Hoyt	20.00
Mrs. F. Sydting	4.00
C. Sydting	4.00
John Sydting	2.00

Greenpoint Hospital

Mary T. Logan	$5.00
Joseph Niederigger	5.00
Miss Emily Brophy	5.00
John Carroll	2.00
Miss Regina Bannon	5.00
Elizabeth Fox	5.00
Mr. and Mrs. M. Lally	25.00
Miss Lundy	5.00
Miss K. Molloy	6.00
A. W. Utecht	$3.00

Hausman Street

Edward Gilgan	$10.00
Mrs. McKillop	20.00
Peter Goodman	12.00
Mrs. Tarsney McMahon	15.00
Joseph Kelly	5.00
Mr. and Mrs. Ed. Nagle	5.00
Mr. and Mrs. Patrick Spellman	2.00
Daniel O'Loane	20.00
Charles Metzger	5.00
Mr. and Mrs. Quinlan	46.00
John Schayer	5.00
Francis J. Armstrong	2.00
Mr. and Mrs. A. Malone	2.00

Hausman Street

John Armstrong	5.00
Mr. and Mrs. H. Reilly	5.00
Mary Kelly and Family	20.00
Mrs. Johanna Euston	5.00
Mary Cahill	5.00
Madaline McSweeney	5.00
Mary Sharkey	2.00
Mr. and Mrs. William Dougherty	5.00
Margaret Lynch	5.00
Fitzgerald Family	15.00
Edward Flynn	5.00
Robert Mulhern	5.00
Denis Ansbro and Family	5.00
John McCann	9.00
Denis Hogan and Family	3.00
Philip Walsh	1.00
Thomas Carney	5.00
Thomas Charles	5.00
L. Lynagh	2.00
William Hagen	5.00
Mrs. G. Frank	3.00
John Whalen	2.00
Mr. and Mrs. Edward Hannon	5.00
M. Butler	10.00
Patrick McShane	25.00
Michael Hillary	5.00
Kathleen Hillary	1.00
Mr. and Mrs. Jos. Nolan	3.00
Louis Wannemeyer	5.00
Mr. and Mrs. M. Nolan	5.00
Thomas Reidy	20.00
Hugh O'Donnell	5.00
Mr. and Mrs. Holt	2.00
Mary Hurley	3.00
Mrs. Cath. Hurley	25.00
Mr. and Mrs. Peter Olsen	5.00
Howard Olsen	2.00

Hausman Street

In Memory of

Aron Ingram	5.00
Archie Kenny	5.00
John Besterney	5.00
James Kilroy	20.00
Wm. Hartman	20.00
Frederick Carlin	5.00
Mrs. John Lang	5.00
Mr. and Mrs. Truesdale	5.00
Martin Quinlan	5.00
Terence Foley	2.00
Mrs. Charles Farrar	10.00
Mrs. J. Sammon	5.00
Bernard O'Donnell	10.00
Mrs. F. Roehrich	25.00
Mrs. J. H. Johnson	3.00
John W. Crilley	2.00
Emil J. Roerich	2.00
Harry A. Crilley	5.00
Mrs. T. McCloy	3.00
Thos. Butler and Family	3.00
Mrs. Francis Carolan	15.00
Mrs. G. R. Brown	5.00
Louis Devlin	3.00
Philip Lannick	5.00
Bailey Lorensberg	5.00
Mr. and Mrs. E. King	10.00
A. J. Connolly	10.00
Mrs. Parthesius	10.00
Mrs. Thomas Dempsey	5.00
Mrs. K. Martin	2.00
Miss Cecelia Parthesius	5.00

Herbert Street

In Memory of

Mrs. Ann Glinnen	$25.00
Hugh O'Rourke	10.00
The Misses Annie and Mary Glinnen	25.00
John J. Kerrigan	20.00

Herbert Street

Arthur Schuler 4.00
James Lonergan 1.00
Angela Tinnes 25.00
Catherine Donohue 25.00
Philip Spanpanata 1.00
Josephine Segretto 10.00
Joseph Keiviecienski 3.00
Hugh McGovern 5.00
William Daniels 20.00
Frank Sisco 2.00
William Sisco 5.00
Miss Mae Sisco 20.00
John Gorski and Family.....15.00
Charles Monahan and
    Family 50.00
William P. Murphy 50.00
William J. Murphy 25.00
Helen Murphy 5.00
Ann Mullaney 10.00
Albert Ignatz 40.00
William Kelly 5.00
Albert Burt 25.00
William Yengel 2.00
John McLinden 10.00
Mary McLinden 5.00
Margaret McLinden 5.00
Patrick Murphy 2.00
Patrick Corbey 3.00
Mary Corbey 3.00
Mrs. E. Hunt 10.00
Irene Murphy 3.00
Bonaventure D'Ascoli 5.00
David Flannery 5.00
Patrick Flannery 5.00
Sebastian Serio 3.00
Joseph McNally 5.00
Charles McDonough 5.00
Mary Mayer 2.00
Mrs. Anastasia Acker 5.00

Herbert Street

Mr. Anthony Ronca 3.00
Miss Eleanor Formato 2.00
Mrs. Mary Ferrera 2.00
Mary Mulhern 5.00
Nellie Donohue 2.00
Catherine Donohue 1.00

Humboldt Street

Michael Nial $10.00
Daniel Robinson 2.00
Mr. and Mrs. Philip J.
    Bohne, Jr. 10.00
Philip and Barbara
    Bohne, Sr. 30.00
Louis Hugenheimer 5.00
Nicolas Matera 2.00
Thomas Quinn 5.00
James Russell 3.00
Anna Decker 13.00
Martin Conroy 3.00
In Memory of
    Thomas Conroy 2.00
    Mary Callahan 10.00
    Mrs. Ellen Trousdell 35.00
    Mrs. Mary Ann Murphy... 5.00
    Peter J. Crean 5.00
    Mary Connelly 5.00
    Marie Kunkel 5.00
    Mark Gilmartin 2.00
James Kane 5.00
Anna Whalen 2.00
Thomas Murphy 2.00
George Canty 3.00
George Wohlmaker 2.00
Edward Doyle 5.00
Jacob Hoffmann 5.00
Forrest B. Nott 15.00
Elizabeth Nott 2.00
George Smith 6.00
James Doran 5.00

Humboldt Street

Elizabeth Tiederman	5.00
Terence Phelan and Patrick Cunningham	25.00
Charles Reardon	5.00
George Reardon	3.00
Michael Noonan	5.00
Mary Noonan	21.00
George Cronin	3.00
Patrick Walsh	5.00
Michael Conley	5.00
Daniel Kraics	3.00
John Jeski	2.00
Stanley Wilenski	3.00
Nicholas Korcz	1.00
Thomas Bowen	1.00
Eugene Morahan and Family	30.00
Cornelius Fitzpatrick	2.00
Ellen Fitzpatrick	1.00
Thomas Loftus	2.00
Thomas Loftus, Jr.	1.00
Mary Loftus	2.00
Edward McCarthy	2.00
William Nott	3.00
John Bourke	1.00
James Bourke	2.00
Roland Wares	5.00
Mary Gruenberg	3.00
Anna Goller	1.00
James Kissane	1.00
Edward J. Coogan	5.00
John O'Brien	1.00
Joseph Munnie	2.00
Edward J. Coogan	20.00
James McEnroe	10.00
Thomas Flynn	3.00
Ellen Monahan	5.00
Rose Heil	3.00
Henry Kekeisen	2.00

Humboldt Street

Edward Bopp	3.00
Mrs. S. Walshak	2.00
Mr. and Mrs. Glennin	5.00
Helen Walshak	3.00
R. Schlieman	2.00
Rose Papke	5.00
Peter R. Crean	5.00
Ann C. Crean	5.00
Mrs. Guilmartin	7.00
Nellie Ford	20.00
Patrick Connelly	5.00
Henry Kunkel	5.00
Mrs. A. Johnson	17.00
James A. Reilly	4.00
Anna Hulse	2.00
Mr. and Mrs. M. Durkin	20.00
Bessie Conlon	5.00
George Leonard	1.00
James J. Cain	2.00
Mr. and Mrs. J. P. Crean	10.00
William Hughes	2.00
Mrs. Helen Dunphy	5.00
Mrs. Elizabeth Chandler	2.00
Baby Joseph McCabe	1.00
Felix Spank	3.00
G. Gressing	2.00

Jackson Street

Mrs. M. Meehan & Family	$5.00
Mr. and Mrs. W. Stubbs	2.00
Thomas Kennedy	30.00
Patrick F. Clancy & Family	65.00
John Slattery	35.00
Frank Segrave	35.00
Francis P. Ward	25.00
Myles Ward	10.00
Myles F. Ward	10.00
Frank Kraemer	5.00
Hugh McKee	1.00
Thomas Havican	1.00

Jackson Street

James Travers	5.00
Thomas Meaghers	5.00
Thomas Mulhern	2.00
Mrs. Mary Schuhlein	5.00
Mrs. Francis J. Carroll	5.00
Edward Elder	5.00
Katherine Meagher	5.00
Anna C. Meagher	5.00
Catherine Lynch	5.00

Jewell Street

Mrs. Miller	$2.00
Mrs. Daushansha	5.00
Mrs. Rocklein	2.00
Mrs. Benedickt	3.00
Margaret Schilling	1.00
Mary Sarosy	3.00

Kingland Avenue

J. Nolan	$5.00
George McHugh	5.00
Mrs. Mary Clemens	2.00
Paul Lehr	1.00
James Mullaney	35.00
Thomas Mullaney	10.00
Charles Lehr	5.00
In Memory of	
Charles Daly	5.00
William Farrell	11.00
John Donlon	20.00
John and Mary C.	
Santry	7.00
James Carlin	10.00
Michael McBride	10.00
Mrs. Elizabeth Stippel	15.00
Mrs. Margaret Memmel	3.00
Monsignor H.	
McFadden of Donegal	10.00
Mr. Leavey	20.00
Charles Baker	2.00
John Burns	2.00

Kingsland Avenue

Bridget McHugh	2.00
George Jean	2.00
Mrs. T. Falvey	2.00
Mrs. Mary McDonald	2.00
Jeremiah O'Neill	5.00
Frank O'Neill	2.00
Mrs. Mary O'Grady	5.00
Patrick Behan	5.00
Michael Crispo	2.00
Dominick Gardini	25.00
Joseph Pellegrino	2.00
John J. O'Neill	10.00
Frank Gernert	3.00
Adam Radomski	10.00
Mrs. Lorden	1.00
George Schilling	1.00
Mrs. Cooke	1.00
Michael Donlon	2.00
Timothy Buckley	25.00
Cornelius Considine	5.00
Mary Considine	2.00
Michael Considine	2.00
Cornelius Considine, Jr.	2.00
William Wallace	4.00
Jeremiah McCarthy	5.00
Margaret McCarthy	3.00
Margaret Wallace	1.00
Alice Wallace	1.00
Edward Gillen	2.00
Paul Pierre	1.00
Mrs. John Reilly	5.00
John Roeser	1.00
Patrick Donleavey	3.00
Howard Tilton	1.00
Mrs. Feeley	2.00
Alexander McMullan	5.00
Mrs. Dembowski	1.00
Mrs. Haverty	1.00
Louis Ottamba	1.00

Kingsland Avenue

Anonymous	3.00
Thos. Gavigan	3.00
Thomas McGaffrey	1.00
Andrew Spano	2.00
Arthur Suckow	5.00
John Toland	2.00
Thomas McArdle	4.00
Thomas Slacke	5.00
Michael Muller	5.00
Marie Buchheit	1.00
William Kemp	3.00
Mrs. Mary McMahon and Family	8.00
Patrick McCullagh	3.00
John O'Dea and Family	5.00
Thomas Fondy	2.00
Mary McIntyre	3.00
Alice McConaghy	2.00
Mrs. Catherine McNally	2.00
William McNally	2.00
Thomas Dumas	30.00
John Hughes	3.00
James Smith	2.00
Sam. Giordano	1.00
Thomas Martin	1.00
Joseph Martin	1.00
Guido Ghiggeri	2.00
Joseph Canavan	5.00
Charles Engfer	1.00
Mrs. Brustman	5.00
Henry Brustman	3.00
John Willis	2.00
Thomas McGuiness	2.00
Mrs. Ellen Dougherty	3.00
James McNamara	5.00
Mrs. James McGuire	3.00
John Amber	2.00
John Duane	2.00
Martin Rafferty	5.00

Kingsland Avenue

Michael Watson	5.00
Michael Salvatore	1.00
Ralph Newton	1.00
John McShane	5.00
Michael Costello	5.00
William Ryan	5.00
Thomas McGlynn, Sr.	5.00
James McGlynn	5.00
John McHugh	3.00
Matthew Lally	3.00
Daniel Timoney	5.00
Brian McShea	2.00
Mrs. Anna Buckley	2.00
John Buckley	2.00
William F. Buckley	2.00
Thomas Buckley	2.00
Mrs. Faint	1.00
Leo Jablonski	3.00
Richard McConnel	1.00
Alvin Wood	5.00
John Reilly	2.00
John Coyle	15.00
Edward Callan	25.00
Chris. Schwerd	5.00
Bernard H. Riley	5.00
Patrick Martin	5.00
Frank Merino	2.00
Mrs. Zweier	15.00
Michael Brady	5.00
John B. Connolly	5.00
John Stephan	2.00
George Walker	2.00
Cornelius Harty	3.00
Anthony Ferzola	2.00
Joseph Supino	2.00
James Villiano	1.00
Stephen White	3.00
Rose Laux	3.00
In honour of St. Teresa	8.00

Kingsland Avenue

Joseph Maher	5.00
George Catterson	5.00
Mrs. Carr	2.00
Matt. Plunkett	10.00
Mrs. Julia Gott	2.00
Joseph Hannifin	2.00
Vincent Hannifin	1.00
William White	3.00
Mrs. F. Meehan	2.00
William McGee	20.00
Thomas Farrell	5.00
T. Slade	25.00
Miss M. Huether	10.00
George Slade	5.00
Mrs. Elsie Looney	2.00
Frank L. Mellick	2.00
Mrs. E. Boyle	2.00
Mrs. Jackson	3.00
Harry Jackson	2.00
Mrs. M. Santry	5.00

Leonard Street

Mrs. Haight	$3.00
Anna Fogarty	3.00
Robert Munnie	2.00
Mrs. Margaret Madigan	15.00
Mrs. Meadows	5.00

Lorimer Street

Mary Higgins	$5.00
Paul Harding	5.00
Joseph Smith	5.00
Mrs. Annie Tuebner	5.00
Frank Reilly	2.00
John Maloney	3.00
James Murray	5.00
Mr. and Mrs. Henry Schneffer	2.00
Mr. and Mrs. J. Byrne	2.00
Mary Lewis	1.00

Lombardy Street

Laurence Spellman	$25.00
Matthew Plunkett	25.00
Charles Beecher	5.00
Mrs. Schreck	3.00
Severino Magnani	25.00
Rose Franchi	1.00
Martin Hesselberg	2.00
Mrs. Matilda Ruprecht	3.00
Mrs. Donohue	2.00
Mrs. Mary Jacob	5.00
Mr. and Mrs. J. Currie	5.00
Charles Stothart	3.00

Meserole Avenue

John Manly	$3.00
William Call	5.00

Manhattan Avenue

Edward Oldis	$2.00
In Memory of	
Margaret Connolly	5.00
James Connolly	5.00
Robert Gordan	2.00
J. M. Grady & Sons	10.00
Mrs. McAvoy	2.00

Morgan Avenue

J. Croudle	$20.00
Michael Graham	25.00
William Wentz	2.00
John Courtade	10.00
Thomas Griffin	5.00
James O'Shea	45.00
Mr. and Mrs. J. Smith	10.00
Mrs. Hawkins	2.00
William Rogers	2.00
Albion Curry	5.00
Martin Hughes	3.00
George H. Marshall	2.00
George McCann	3.00
Morris Lynch	5.00
Anthony Mullady	1.00

Morgan Avenue

In Memory of

Alice Smith	5.00
John Lydon	2.00
John Smith	3.00
Mr. and Mrs. W. P. Duffy	10.00
Catherine Moran	5.00
James Larkin	25.00
Loretta Brown	2.00
John Beecher	5.00
Andrew Pavera	1.00
John Dwyer	2.00
Mrs. Malone	2.00
John Lehr	5.00
Daniel Donohue	2.00
Charles Heidt	3.00
Mrs. Duffy	3.00
Peter Kelly	5.00
S. Millar	25.00
Matthew Huber	3.00
Wm. McCrory and Family	5.00
Catherine Neenan	1.00
Joseph Millar	2.00
Andrew and Mrs. Neenan	7.00
Kieran Martin	2.00
J. Ronan	5.00
Frank Bucher	1.00
Daniel Goodman	3.00
Michael Curran	2.00
Alexander Kissane	1.00
Fred Horn	2.00
James White	5.00
Thomas McManus	5.00
John Labriola	1.00
John Walsh	5.00
George F. Cassin	5.00
John Scarry	5.00
Mrs. Cooney	2.00
Frank Calandriello	3.00

Morgan Avenue

Nellie Ray	3.00
Catherine Grady	2.00
John Colleran	2.00
Hugh Gorman	15.00
Jeremiah Grimes	26.00
Mr. and Mrs. Schoenstein	5.00
John O'Dwyer	2.00
William Clair	2.00
Clarence Cronin	1.00
Mrs. Mary Cronin	1.00
James Neville	2.00
William Melville	3.00
In honour of St. Teresa	3.00
Mrs. Mary McQuillan	5.00
Patrick Griffin	10.00
Michael Graham	25.00
John McHugh	2.00
Mrs. Lucy Hanrahan	35.00
Cross Family	2.00
John Horan	2.00
Patrick Moran	1.00
Michael Moran	1.00
John Lynd	2.00
Mr. and Mrs. J. Roman	10.00
George Odgen	2.00
Anna Larkin	3.00
Mr. & Mrs. J. McLoughlin	5.00
Hopkins Family	10.00
Joseph Grassert	5.00
Thomas Stanton	2.00
Patrick O'Dea	5.00
John McAllister	2.00
Edward Fitzpatrick	5.00
Mr. and Mrs. Thomas Gorman	25.00
In Memory of Michael and Nora Gorman	5.00
McGaugh Family	5.00
Catherine Neary	5.00

Morgan Avenue

Mr. and Mrs. Wm. Dunn	10.00
Mrs. B. Martin	2.00
James O'Donnell	2.00
James Gorman	5.00
Mr. and Mrs. Hennessy	1.00
Mr. and Mrs. Thos. E. Rohan	5.00
Mr. and Mrs. Thos. T. Rohan	5.00
Mr. and Mrs. John Brown	5.00
Thomas Walsh	2.00
Barry Family	20.00
Michael Rohan	5.00
John Coyne	5.00
William Hoch	2.00
Raymond Cullen	20.00
P. Morris	5.00
Mrs. Matthew McEvoy	3.00
Mrs. McKeegan	2.00
John Lentz	2.00
James Flannagan	25.00
Mrs. Teresa Tierney	25.00
Anthony Kopher	5.00
Harold Sandin	14.00
Harold Sandin, Jr.	1.00
Bernard Wannemeyer	5.00
Mr. & Mrs. Myles Spears	10.00
Marion Spears	5.00
Thomas Spears	5.00
Patrick Walker	13.00
William Neidhardt	13.00
James C. Higgins	5.00
Mrs. Mary Peabody	2.00
Wm. Fitzgerald & Family	25.00
John H. Nicholsen	40.00
Catherine Nicholson	1.00
Mrs. Helen Hyland	2.00
Mrs. Sweeney	2.00
William Caldwell	5.00

Morgan Avenue

Mr. and Mrs. Jas. Deery	5.00
Edward McGrath	5.00
Marie Tierney	5.00
Mrs. Jas. Deery	20.00
Mrs. W. Smith	20.00
Mr. and Mrs. Catterson	25.00
Josephine Crawford	15.00
Mr. and Mrs. J. Hennery	2.00
Christine Fleckenstein	2.00
Denis P. Devere	2.00
Sylvester Proctor	2.00
Angeline Seiler	3.00
Mary Nicholsen	20.00
Robert Minary	5.00
Mary D. Goodman	1.00

Monitor Street

In Memory of

Richard and Mary O'Neil	5.00
Mary Veronica O'Neill	5.00
Martin Mannion	2.00
Harry Ward	25.00
Mrs. Mary Clayton	5.00
Edward J. Murray	5.00
J. P. Courtney	10.00
James Gonnoud	5.00
John Schweitzer	5.00
Mrs. Catherine Langville	3.00
George Grobe	2.00
James Dooley	5.00
John Churchill	10.00
Honora Collins	15.00
Michael Ward	10.00
James V. Crilly	$15.00
James V. Crilly, Jr.	5.00
Mrs. Alice Cox and Family	10.00
Thomas Cox	2.00
Peter Harten	2.00
Frank Caldwell	1.00
Thomas J. Cummings	20.00

Monitor Street

David Cain	5.00
Mrs. Mary Murphy	10.00
Frank Murphy	5.00
Gilbert McGregor	7.00
Margaret Kiernan	5.00
Sylvester McGrath	3.00
Mrs. Annie Lannon	5.00
Helen Lannon	1.00
Matthew Traynor	2.00
David Creaven	2.00
Martin Corbett	2.00
Mrs. Mary Corbett	5.00
Mrs. Ellen Moore	2.00
James O'Malley	5.00
Malcolm McCambridge	25.00
Patrick McAllister	5.00
Joseph McAllister	3.00
Robert J. Etherson	5.00
Mary Keehan	105.00
Fred. Schwind	5.00
Edward Levie	2.00
Peter Fitzgerald	5.00
John Kennedy and Family	12.00
William Veit	10.00
Mrs. Margaret Moylan	5.00
The Courtney Family	50.00
William J. Courtney	10.00
J. Corbett and Family	10.00
Miss Margaret L. Walker	30.00
Mrs. P. Kennedy	18.00
Dorothy Kivlin	5.00
Mrs. Murray	20.00
John Greene	2.00
John Cornell	3.00
Harry Orff	1.00
Wylfred Orff	1.00
Henry Kivlin	3.00
Howard V. Kivlin	5.00
John Quinn and Family	30.00

Monitor Street

James McNiff	35.00
Matthew Maloney	15.00
John Gough	5.00
John McEvoy	15.00
Maurice Kinsella	10.00
Mrs. M. Cummisky	5.00
Joseph Jockel	3.00
Henry Martin	5.00
Henry F. Hill	20.00
Mrs. F. Walker	10.00
Mrs. Catherine Duignan	2.00
William Breason	5.00
James H. Murray	5.00
Mrs. Mary Marshall	3.00
John C. Maher	75.00
Timothy Shea	2.00
William Tyack	2.00
Edward Johnston	5.00
Patrick Loughlin	20.00
Mr. & Mrs. Francis Brady	35.00
Stephen McDermott	5.00
Miss Winifred Gibbons	
Mrs. Loretta Ward	5.00
N. A. Hoffman & Family	5.00
Patrick H. Heaney	5.00
James Teague	5.00
Mrs. James G. Sutphin	20.00
Patrick Kennedy	3.00
John Schmidt	5.00
Denis Ryan	20.00
Mrs. Mary Donovan	3.00
Mrs. M. Boyle	10.00
George Basso	10.00
Mrs. Heege	7.00
Miss Kaeding	2.00
Thomas Quinn	3.00
Miss Hein	10.00
Mrs. Mary R. Beareck	5.00
Charles Heege	4.00

Monitor Street

Mr. and Mrs. J. Crilly	25.00
James V. Crilly	5.00
Mrs. Hefferan	2.00
Mary Kekut	2.00
Mrs. Teresa Wassmer	2.00
John Coleman & Family	25.00
George Coleman	2.00
Agnes Coleman	2.00
Veronica Coleman	1.00
August Strumpfler	5.00
Michael Kunz	2.00
Benie Citero	1.00
George Hedberg, Jr.	3.00
Eugene Slattery	5.00
Philip Taggart	30.00
Mary Taggart	5.00
Dominic Rotella	5.00
William Mattes	1.00
Mrs. Mae Callahan	2.00
John Gilroy	5.00
Catherine Miller	1.00
John McCormick	5.00
Ellen Rooney	1.00
Agnes Mannion	1.00
John Lucas	1.00
Charles N. Jantz	2.00
Edward Cusack	5.00
Mrs. Kerwick	3.00
Frank Kiernan	5.00
Alexander Cameron	5.00
John J. Mooney	50.00
Elizabeth McDermott	2.00
Mrs. Sarah Coyne	3.00
James Butler	2.00
Daniel Monahan	3.00
Lester Perry	5.00
Eugene Freuhwirth	5.00
Teresa Fruehwirth	2.00
Catherine Fruehwirth	2.00

Monitor Street

Edward Fruerwirth	1.00
John McGrath	25.00
Edward Richards	3.00
David Acker	30.00
Thomas O'Donnell	3.00
William O'Donnell	1.00
Patrick Heaney	10.00
Mrs. Mary O'Brien	5.00
John Gillen	5.00
George J. Fitzsimons	3.00
Harry Fitzsimons	2.00
Mrs. Byrne	5.00
James Laffey	5.00
Henry Archambault	2.00
John C. Gorhman	2.00
George Gaffney	5.00
George Price	5.00
Mr. and Mrs. Chas. J. Feist	3.00
Miss Florence Feist	2.00
Master Joseph W. Feist	1.00
Frank Segretto	1.00
Jean Cook	1.00
Mrs. Sarah Cook	2.00
Alice Daniels	5.00
John P. Runyon	3.00
Frank Blanchfield	5.00
William Ewald	2.00
William Glading	3.00
Michael Clancy	5.00
John McCabe	1.00
William A. Jones	10.00
Thomas J. Kilmartin	35.00
William T. Kilmartin	5.00
John S. E. Kilmartin	5.00
Lillian Kilmartin (In Memory of her Mother)	1.00
Daniel Cooney	5.00
Charles Hoepper	2.00

Monitor Street

William Mohnkern	5.00
Michael Cosgrove	5.00
William Donohue	2.00
John Croudle	5.00
Ferdinand Bock, Sr.	2.00
Patrick Faulkner	10.00
Martin Molloy	5.00
Patrick McCartin	5.00

Meeker Avenue

Jacob Blesser	$10.00
Thomas Carey	5.00
Mrs. John P. Wallace	5.00
John Scholl	3.00
John Grant	2.00
In Memory of	
William Drohan	5.00
Mary Walsh	
Margaret Slammon	
John McMillan	5.00
Ellen Smith	30.00
P. J. Boylan	25.00
Edward Glinnen	10.00
George Long	10.00
John McGrane, Jr.	2.00
Patrick O'Neill	5.00
Mrs. Mary Craddock	5.00
Mrs. Joseph Kortkamp	5.00
Matthew Kortkamp	2.00
Mrs. J. McMillan	5.00
James A. Lamb	5.00
Margaret Smith and	
E. J. Flynn	20.00
Hubert Neal	20.00
Mrs. William McGhee	20.00
Edward and Esther	
Gallagher	20.00
Mrs. N. Flannagan	25.00
Mrs. Hamill	10.00
Patrick McGrattan	5.00

Meeker Avenue

Mrs. P. Gengler	10.00
Edward Morris	5.00
Catherine Mullane	5.00
William Etherson	5.00
Alexander McKay	5.00
Lawrence Murtha	5.00
Mrs. Josephine Kelly	3.00
William Kelly	2.00
Remembrance of Edna	
and Edward Meyer	3.00
Anna Walsh	2.00
John Alcott	5.00
Edward F. Bickel	8.00
Mary Krans	1.00
John McGrane	15.00
John Monahan	1.00
Cornelius Caulfield	2.00
Margaret Brown	1.00
Michael Dirkes	10.00
Henry Philips	3.00
Peter Mullin	5.00
Thomas Mullin	6.00
John Gavin	5.00
Louis Bajodek	1.00
William Hesselberg and	
Family	10.00
Mrs. C. Storm	2.00
George Alpers	5.00
William Hynes	5.00
John McAuliffe	30.00
William F. Schneider	40.00
Edward Fitzgerald	3.00
Van Nostrand Family	10.00
Joseph Kortkamp	3.00
Mrs. L. Routledge	10.00
Mrs. G. Lamneck	10.00
Mary Torpey	2.00
William Dunn	5.00
William Harrison	2.00

Meeker Avenue

Carl C. Henriksen	2.00
Joseph Guie	3.00
Matthew Foley	25.00
A Friend	5.00
James Curry	5.00
Michael Beatrice	1.00
Pasquale Antonia	1.00
Patrick O'Connor	20.00
Mrs. H. Coleman	2.00
Patrick Mulvihill	4.00
P. J. Stenger	45.00
Mrs. Mary Gorman	3.00
Mrs. Cath. McCormick	1.00
Miss Emma Schneider	1.00
John Dunnigan	2.00
Rose Dunnigan	1.00
Mary Dunnigan	2.00
Miss Emma Perry	1.00
James Twiggs	10.00
Miss Elizabeth Murray	3.00
Thomas Elliott	2.00
Hugh Ferris	30.00
Mrs. Delia Gately	5.00
Leonard Wendel	10.00
Mrs. Margaret Wendel	5.00
Irene Wendel	1.00
John Gardini	4.50
Hugh Collins	5.00
James J. Sullivan	5.00
Anna Cavanagh	5.00
William Cavanagh	5.00
Madeline Heuther	10.00
Wiliam McGee	3.00
Thomas Mullen	6.00

Nassau Avenue

James McNeil	$2.00
Mr. and Mrs. Wm. Bealler	5.00
Samuel Winters	3.00
Mr. and Mrs. Michael Doyle	5.00

Nassau Avenue

In Memory of

Rosanna Finnerty	10.00
James Higgins	3.00
Patrick Reilly	3.00
Cornelius Mahoney	10.00
Thomas Ohrts	5.00
John and Cath. Weber	5.00
James White and Mary Campbell	7.00
Mrs. T. Foley	5.00
Louise Delaney	10.00
Willis Hamilton Miner	5.00
Edward Shannon	10.00
Martin Kelleher	2.00
Owen Moran	5.00
James McCaffery	3.00
James McCaffery, Jr.	2.00
Mrs. A. Wahler	3.00
Thomas Hourican	15.00
Michael Hourican	2.00
Patrick Garvin	1.00
Michael Maher	2.00
M. McLoughlin	3.00
Joseph Comiskey	1.00
Robert Reischer	3.00
Mrs. Amelia Neumann	1.00
Adam Schmitt	30.00
Bart Roman	2.00
Larry Mannion	1.00
John A. Painting	25.00
Cath. Painting	5.00
Michael Hernan	25.00
Cath. Hernan	2.00
Mrs. M. Hernan	3.00
John Reilly	2.00
Joseph Ackley	15.00
Rudolph Kandra	3.00
Jacobina Klein	2.00
Jeremiah Staeger	5.00

Nassau Avenue

William McDermott	2.00
Louis Benson	3.00
Frank Frey	3.00
Thomas Norris	5.00
Peter Mannion	5.00
Patrick Croudle	30.00
William Graham	5.00
James Hansen	5.00
R. Remmers	2.00
Joseph P. Carlin	2.00
George Zahn	1.00
Owen Molloy	30.00
Margaret Mallory	2.00
John Latelle	1.00
Mr. and Mrs. Peter Kriedler	3.00
John McCambridge	2.00
John McAllister	5.00
Martha Reilly	2.00
D. Quinn	5.00
Patrick McKenna	3.00
Mrs. A. Quinlan	2.00
Mrs. McGill	5.00
Mary Kelly	5.00
Dominic Coane	10.00
James Shannon	30.00
John Hickey	2.00
John Huber	1.00
Frank McGowan	5.00
Stanley Gaynor	5.00
Andrew Washach	7.00
Bernard McDevitt	2.00
Denis Quille	10.00
Mrs. E. Shannon	10.00
John Hawkins	2.00
James Quille	3.00
Lucy Conlon	23.00
Elizabeth Kelly	3.00
Samuel Conlon	2.00
Rosetta Rulhil	2.00

Nassau Avenue

William Melville	6.00
Robert Melville	2.00
Mrs. Chas. Rhan	1.00
Frank Taylor	5.00
Harry Dougherty	3.00
Mrs. Frank Dougherty	3.00
Patrick Closkey	3.00
Mary Connors	2.00
Anna Gardiner	2.00
Ellen Jaeger	3.00
Mr. and Mrs. Tobin	11.00
Patrick Monohan	5.00
James Pickett	2.00
Mrs. Anna Gerhardt	35.00
Mrs. Colberg and Family	28.00
Mr. and Mrs. John Barry	5.00
John Barry, Jr.	2.00
Keenan White	3.00
Patrick Keene	3.00
Eric Nelson	2.00
William Delaney	5.00
John Maree and Family	23.00
Philip Maree	5.00
Thomas Marra	5.00
William Schmelzle	5.00
James Sullivan	5.00
Michael Kenny	3.00
Mrs. James Mullaney	20.00
Katherine Mullaney	5.00
Philip Ferst	2.00
William Dombrowsky	5.00
Joseph Fagan	1.00
Michael Morek	1.00
Catherine Stewart	5.00
Edward Newman	25.00
John Boyle	5.00
John Normandy	5.00
James Courtney	5.00
C. L. Barton	25.00

Nassau Avenue

F. D. Sembler 25.00
Mr. and Mrs. Schall 5.00
Patrick Purtell 5.00
John Mahoney 10.00
Mrs. E. Broderick 2.00
Mrs. Frueh 1.00
Owen Caffrey 25.00
Joseph Conroy 3.00
Mrs. Mary Gavin 3.00
John H. Waldron 5.00

North Henry Street

Mr. and Mrs. William
   Bunden $5.00
Mrs. McDonald and Sons 10.00
Mr. and Mrs. J. Butler 30.00
Annetta Butler 2.00
Philip Schutta 1.00
Delia Conroy 7.00
Thomas Flynn 5.00
Mr. and Mrs. P. Conlon 5.00
Robert Schutta 1.00
In Memory of
  Mr. and Mrs. John Rohr 20.00
  Thomas Curry 5.00
  Philip Brady 5.00
  Mr. and Mrs. J. P.
  Corcoran 30.00
  Cath. Reardon 5.00
  Jeremiah Hannefin 5.00
  Mrs. A. Hedberg 2.00
  Catherine Farnon 20.00
  Mr. and Mrs. J. Philips 5.00
  Grace Ditterman 2.00
  Joseph Norton 2.00
  Elizabeth V. Meyers 5.00
  John Cruise 5.00
Maria Rohr 5.00
Mr. and Mrs. G. Lynch 5.00
Bernard Fagan 2.00

North Henry Street

Alice Fagan 2.00
Mrs. Mary Harnest 10.00
Mrs. E. Stevens 5.00
Wm. Hobbs and Family 20.00
Mrs. Mary Byrne 2.00
Adolph Herdenrich 5.00
Rose Bruen 1.00
Mrs. McKeon 2.00
Mrs. Mary Kerwin 30.00
John Ward 5.00
Stephen White and Family 50.00
Eugene White 2.00
L. C. Westrich 5.00
Mrs. Mary Rodgers 5.00
Patrick Burk 2.00
Mr. and Mrs. J. Slowey 5.00
Thomas Egan 2.00
James Hanley 3.00
John Scharl 5.00
William Meinhardt 1.00
Anthony Finochio 1.00
Albert Finochio 1.00
Mr. and Mrs. J. Walker 5.00
Mr. and Mrs. J. Schlicht 5.00
A. Hulse and Family 10.00
M. Walsh and Family 10.00
Sophie Van Ness 2.00
John Burt 1.00
Mr. and Mrs. G. Lilgequist 10.00
Estelle Corcoran 5.00
Lucy Corcoran 5.00
Mr. and Mrs. J. Kenny 10.00
Mr. and Mrs. Jos. Dee 5.00
Harry Clayton 2.00
Mr. and Mrs. D. Moran 3.00
Mr. and Mrs. J. Stevens 2.00
Rita Rombel 2.00
William Simpson 2.00
Edward Farnon 5.00

North Henry Street

Michael Coffey	5.00
John Dolan	5.00
Bernard McMahon	25.00
Andrew Goetz	10.00
Mrs. George Schulte	2.00
John Flood	10.00
Edward Morris	20.00
James Twomlin	20.00
Julia Kerwin	10.00
M. Daly	5.00
Benjamin Potts	25.00
Miss Mae Lennon	10.00
Alice Kerwin	10.00
Mary Clements	7.00
Mrs. Harry Sweeney	25.00
Mrs. Cronnin	20.00
Michael Looney	3.00
Mr. Williams	1.00
Mary Fallon	2.00
James Clemens	2.00
Arthur Purcell	20.00
Genevieve Purcell	1.00
William Moran	5.00
James Murray	5.00
John Nagler	5.00
Edna Habenrich	7.00
John Slowey	5.00
Nicholas Di Stefano	2.00
Louis Frazetti	2.00
Joseph Frazetti	2.00
Charles O'Neil	15.00
Bernard McMahon	15.00
Martin Shannon	5.00
Thomas Kennedy	3.00
Mrs. Julia Repp	20.00
Daniel Phelan	25.00
Michael and Cath. Corbett	26.00
Cornelius Neenan	3.00
Miss Mary Clemens	10.00

North Henry Street

Mr. Thomas J. Creamer and Family	75.00
Dominic Besogno and Family	10.00
Mrs. William Alter	5.00
Martin Giff	5.00
James Giff	2.00
William Byrne	10.00
William Smith	5.00
Mr. and Mrs. E. Walters	5.00
James Slowey	5.00
P. Sullivan	3.00
Denis Sullivan	5.00
Wm. Moran and Family	5.00
Mrs. Margaret Higgins	1.00
Carey Bros.	5.00
Joseph Tomlin	10.00
Emma Rohr	5.00
James Russell	2.00

Newton Street

Andrew McQueeny	$1.00
Leonard F. Sultan	7.00
Mrs. M. Murphy	2.00
Thomas Broderick	3.00
John Gallavan	2.00
Felix McGarty	5.00
Timothy O'Brien	3.00
Mrs. Anna May	5.00
Philip Brady	2.00
William Mulligan	5.00
Walter Bates	5.00
Edward Cummings	2.00
Mrs. A. Moriarity	3.00
Cecilia Moriarity	2.00
George Schnurr	2.00
In Memory of Michael Cummings	3.00
Mrs. Mary Crans	3.00
Mrs. Rutledge	5.00

Newell Street

Mr. La Rosa $1.00
In Memory of
  Bridget Casey 5.00
A. Rouse 5.00
P. Rouse 2.00
Alexander Radagan 2.00
Mr. and Mrs. J. Decker........25.00
George Decker 25.00
Mrs. Lattner 2.00
Mr. and Mrs. A.
  McCambridge 5.00
Mr. and Mrs. J. M. Werner 2.00
Mr. and Mrs. J. Broderick 2.00
Grace Daniels 1.00
Mr. and Mrs. Brogan 3.00
Mr. and Mrs. H. Eastwood 3.00
Mr. and Mrs. Patrick
  Hannon 5.00
Catherine Kiernan 4.00
Mr. and Mrs. J. Gaynor........ 5.00
Mrs. Ficken 1.00
Mr. and Mrs. Liddane 2.00
Campbell Family 10.00
Mrs. Farrell 3.00
Robert McAllister 5.00
Mrs. Catherine Miller 2.00
Owen Caffery 25.00
Mrs. S. Wisnieski 2.00
Marie Wisnieski 2.00
Josephine Wisnieski 1.00

Norman Avenue

Miss Mary Flood $10.00
Mrs. M. Pratt and Family 15.00
James Cherry 10.00
Michael Stanton 3.00
Mary C. Donnelly (In
  Memory of my Father
  and Mother) 110.00
Catherine Murphy 2.00

Oakland Street

Joseph Kujawa 2.00
Mrs. Jackowski 5.00
Mrs. Duffy 5.00
Harry Adolfson 3.00
Mrs. Mary Smith 3.00
John Russell 1.00
Mrs. Brascher 1.00
Robert Middleton 2.00
Martha Reardon 3.00
Agnes Reardon 1.00
Charles Tarsney 3.00
In Memory of
  Michael and John Coyne 2.00
Mrs. J. Quinn 2.00
John Quinn 2.00

Old Wood Point Road

John Downey $10.00
Julia O'Brien 2.00

Orient Avenue

William Moore $30.00
Thomas Curran 45.00
Joseph Weisse 5.00

Richardson Street

Andrew Rossi and Family...$10.00
Joseph Sweet 5.00
Garret Whalen 35.00
Daniel J. Doyle:
  (In Memory of my
  beloved Mother,
  Mary A. Doyle) 5.00
Thomas F. McKeever 10.00
William J. Leahy...................10.00
Elizabeth McDonough:
  (In Memory of Mrs.
  Elizabeth McDonough) ...25.00
William McDonough:
  (In Memory of his
  Mother Mary, and his
  sister Elizabeth) 2.00

Richardson Street

Peter Leahy	2.00
Patrick Lapolla	2.00
Salvatore Caccarola	1.00
Mrs. Ruck	1.00
Mrs. Julia Slater	15.00
Mrs. David Knab	5.00
Miss McCormack	10.00

Russell Street

Joseph P. McGee	$5.00
In Memory of	
Wm. P. Murphy	10.00
James Kelly	5.00
Martin Golden, Sr. and Jr.	5.00
James J. and Matthew Joseph P. Oulette	5.00
Thomas Carroll	1.00
Mrs. Mary Callanan	30.00
Mrs. Kane	3.00
John and Cath. Casey	10.00
John Scanlon	5.00
Johanna Cummings	20.00
Patrick Hines	5.00
Michael Kinsella	5.00
Patrick Meehan	5.00
J. C. Murphy	5.00
Miss Alice Farmer	10.00
Nellie E. Briggs	20.00
Mrs. Griffin	10.00
Thomas Young	10.00
Charles Young	2.00
George Carroll	5.00
John Scanlon	2.00
Michaer Maher	5.00
Joseph Sullivan	2.00
John McAllister	2.00
Daniel Murphy	6.00
Mrs. Margaret Reid	5.00
Patrick McNicholas	5.00

Russell Street

The Misses McDermott	5.00
Joseph Duggan	5.00
John Duggan	5.00
A. I. McGinn	5.00
John Dailey	7.00
Daniel McCauley	5.00
David Pickett	5.00
Margaret Andzis	1.00
William Perry	2.00
Percy Glasco	5.00
John F. Donohue	10.00
John F. Donohue, Jr.	3.00
Maurice Donohue	2.00
Cecilia Kilroy	3.00
Michael O'Rourke	5.00
Marie O'Rourke	27.00
John J. Schutte	15.00
Frank Schutte	70.00
Charles Hennigan	5.00
John Ward	5.00
Mr. Bienert	25.00
Thomas Fitzpatrick	5.00
A. Cross	13.00
James Smith	1.00
Frank Mayo	2.00
Richard Gorman	5.00
John Quinn	25.00
James Hughes	3.00
Thomas Carney	5.00
Joseph Janulevich	2.00
Mrs. Annie Prendeville	3.00
Joseph Schulte	5.00
Nicholas Carolan	2.00
John Walsh	5.00
Mr. and Mrs John Scanlon	5.00
John Schaub	2.00
John Reardon	7.00
Walter P. Casey and Family	40.00

Russell Street

Dr. James B. Tormey 50.00
Michael Conway 2.00
Edward Bailey 3.00
Dr. Frank J. Tarseny 20.00
Mrs. Kate Micucci 10.00
Mrs. Catherine Hedberg 2.00
Patrick Ward 5.00
Mrs. Alice Kelly 2.00
Mrs. Mary Rassiga 3.00
Mrs. Margaret Thompson 2.00
Joseph Clancy 10.00
William Hanousek 5.00
Mrs. Cyriac Du Brul 5.00
Miss Nell Du Brul 5.00
Catherine McGee 5.00
Samuel Darrow 20.00
Mrs. Annie Buckley 2.00
Abraham Birmingham 35.00
L. Devine 45.00
Frank Gormely 10.00
Mrs. Mary Metz 20.00
William Stillwaggon 4.00
E. V. McGolrick, M.D. 25.00
Matthew Healy 20.00
Patrick Ryan 20.00
Thomas McManus 30.00
John C. McManus 10.00
Mrs. T. J. McManus 5.00
Andrew Cortez 2.00
Edwin Navarra 1.00
Michael Quinn 5.00
Catherine Carey and Family 5.00
Bruce Colepaugh 2.00
John Boehmer 1.00
Edward Malgraf 1.00
Patrick Miney 5.00
Margaret Gillespie 5.00
Margaret Dahig 10.00
John Reardon 2.00

Russell Street

James Mahon 3.00
Mrs. Catherine Foley 5.00
Mrs. Monahan 2.00
Delia Walsh 2.00
Frank Ackerman 5.00
Bert Scharf 5.00
Luke Reilly and Family 15.00
Biagio Grieco 10.00
Pasquale Zazzarino 2.00
James Canning 7.00
Leon Berland 5.00
Henry Bornkamp 5.00
Charles Loesel 1.00
August A. Markart 1.00
John Young 2.00
Frank Schneider 10.00
Anna M. Jacobs 5.00
William Campion 3.00
Edward McHugh 3.00
William Albrecht 2.00
Mrs. Arthur Schuler 3.00
Miss Anna Simms 5.00
T. Kelly 2.00
Archibald McGill 3.00
John Kelly 3.00
James Kennelly 2.00
Peter O'Brien 3.00
John Sullivan 2.00
Charles Kerner 2.00
James Feeney 2.00
Martin Carroll 1.00
James Casey 5.00
Mr. and Mrs. Thomas
Gardner 8.00
George Cosgrove 2.00
John Koppenhoefer 13.00
John Koppenhoefer, Jr. 2.00
Leroy Bauman 5.00
John Duhig 12.00

Russell Street

Cornelius McGrath	2.00
Helen Neylan	10.00
George Ott	5.00
Joseph Wilson	10.00
Peter McDermott	5.00
A. Nappi and Family	25.00
John Alisen	5.00
Joseph Kuhl	5.00
Margaret O'Neill	2.00
Patrick White	10.00
Andrew Klarman	2.00
Michael Dempsey	35.00
James P. Dempsey	5.00
John J. Dempsey	5.00
Mrs. Ellen McGee	23.00
Harry Golden	5.00
Simon Hill	20.00
Miss Elizabeth Devine	5.00
Mrs. N. W. Wright	5.00
H. Karges	5.00
John Donohue	5.00
Christopher McKee	10.00
Mrs. Mary O'Neill	5.00
Patrick Daily	7.00
Mr. Gilbert Kelly	3.00
John V. Meehan	2.00
H. O'Hanlon	1.00
Frank Corcoran	10.00

Skillman Avenue

Elizabeth McGrath	$2.00
In Memory of	
John Klernan	5.00

Sutton Street

John Maree	$2.00
Mrs. M. Behringer and	
Mrs. Cath. Behringer-	
Schwallach	22.00
Michael Farrell	3.00
Patrick Lydon	10.00

Sutton Street

Edward Duggan	3.00
Hugh McAuley	1.00
Charles Dougherty	5.00
James Conlon	2.00
Mrs. Pauline Ritter	7.00
Peter Ritter	20.00
William Adamski	3.00
Mrs. Crotty	2.00
Mrs. E. Price	1.00
Edward Machel	5.00
William Hordt	2.00
Francis Kelly	3.00
Maurice Blake	3.00
In Memory of	
Mrs. Cath. Duffy	5.00
Bernard Larkin	2.00
May McCartin	10.00
John Lannon	5.00
Barth. McDonnel	1.00
Joseph A. Dalton	5.00
Thomas McGrane	5.00
James McGill	3.00
Mrs. Thompson	1.00
James Sullivan	2.00
Susanna Roberts	1.00
Maurice Watson	2.00
James Mullaney	2.00
Patrick Cunningham	2.00
John A. Walsh	3.00
John Reilly	3.00
William Plunkett	2.00
William E. McEvoy	2.00
Mr. and Mrs. McCartin	10.00
Jas. Keenan	5.00
John White	3.00
Edward Bermingham	1.00
Denis Goonan	5.00
Mrs. Gunther	1.00
Thomas McClery	1.00

Sutton Street

Ferdinand Eidan	2.00
Thomas J. Sullivan	5.00
Patrick Doherty	3.00
Mrs. Healy	2.00
Mary Roach	3.00
James and Michael McKillop	2.00
Felix McHenry	1.00
Fred Froelich	2.00
Anthony Grego	2.00
Nicholas Nolan	2.00
Jerry Di Giori	2.00
Simon Bourke	5.00
Martin Keane	5.00
John Harley	3.00
Thomas Mullin	2.00
Charles Kerrigan	5.00
Mrs. Hanna	2.00
Mrs. Mary Kennedy	5.00
Charles Vorher	2.00
Walter Delahunty	25.00
Mr. M. Jarvis	3.00
Mr. and Mrs. Patrick Clarke	10.00
Mrs. G. Sisti	3.00
Martin Rohan	5.00
William Barthold	3.00
James McDonnell	7.00
James McDonnell, Jr.	2.00
Thomas Hudson	5.00

Union Avenue

Mrs. Carr	$1.00
Mr. Connors	2.00
Mrs. Connors	2.00
Hugh Connors	1.00
Wienan Family	1.00

Vandervort Street

Patrick Fallon	$10.00
Arthur Thornhill	10.00
Patrick Burke	5.00
William Norris	2.00
Catherine McGuire	1.00
Joseph Farrell	15.00
Goode Family	27.00
John Hynes	27.00
John Hynes, Jr.	3.00
Felix Bramnick	5.00
Frederick Kober	2.00
Sylvester Ahearn	2.00

Van Dam Street

Edward Doherty	$30.00
Walter Lacy	30.00
John McKillop	35.00
Joseph Kittel	1.00
Mrs. Cornelius Logan	5.00
Henry Rhodes	2.00
Mr. Harnett	2.00
George Dewalters	2.00
Mrs. Teresa Gill and Mary T. Gill	22.00
Joseph Zipp	5.00

Withers Street

Dr. Wm. De La Hoyde	$10.00
Nora Curran	2.00
Julia Curran	2.00
James Curran	2.00
George Madigan	5.00
Edward Hoar	5.00
William Rogers	5.00
William Arundel	2.00
William Sherry	2.00
Anna Colgan	2.00
Jacob Schmitt	5.00

Withers Street

In Memory of

Peter Cooney	5.00
Mildred Scongeralla	1.00
Thomas Cooney	3.00
Catherine Cooney	2.00
Anna Crean	20.00
John Wedloch	50.00

Withers Street

In Memory of William

and Elizabeth Stevens	5.00
John Cassidy	10.00
Mrs. Elizabeth McDermott	10.00
George W. Koerner	5.00

$14,069.62

We are profoundly grateful to our people for the generous manifestation of their continued interest in the many activities of our great parish.

CELEBRATION OF ST. CECILIA'S FEAST
NINETEEN HUNDRED AND THIRTY.

The high blue skies of Italy seemed borrowed for the day, its sunshine too, and the chill air of a November sea made no attempt to blow inland. Such a day it was in truth as the little Virgin-Martyr herself might have chosen for gift to her Brooklyn children to inspire and gladden them.

Chime music floated from the tower of St. Cecilia's, the doorways of the church were garlanded and within, the aisles were carpeted in sweetly odorous everygreen and bay-laurel, type of the redolence of the Roman maiden's gentleness, of her fortitude, her suffering and her sanctity.

Up the middle aisle at eleven o'clock came the crossbearer heading a colorful procession of acolytes, visiting Monsignori and clergy. Then came the Deacon, Sub-Deacon and Celebrant of the Mass, clothed in their gorgeous vestments. The sweet-toned organ sounded and the beautifully trained voices of the Boys' Choir broke forth in song, lifting worshippers out of their clay casing entirely to let their free souls for one rapturous moment meet with Cecilia's before the throne of God.

The solemn High Mass was sung this year, as on forty-two previous Feastdays, by the Pastor, Monsignor McGolrick. He was assisted by his curates, Rev. Henry Doheny as Deacon, and Rev. John Krieg as Sub-Deacon. A third curate, Rev. Eugene McLoughlin was the panegyrist.

Within the Sanctuary, sat the Right Rev. Monsignor Ambrose Shumack, Pastor of St. Fidelis', College Point, N. Y., Right Rev. Monsignor Charles Gibney, former Assistant, who is now pastor of the parish of Our Lady of Mt. Carmel, Astoria, L. I., Rev. Francis Uleau, Pastor of St. Bartholemew's, Elmhurst, L. I., Rev. Patrick J. Manton, former Assistant, now Pastor of the parish of St. Teresa of the Little Flower, Brooklyn, Rev. James F. Irwin, former Assistant, now Pastor of Our Lady of Victory Church, Floral Park, L. I. Rev. Peter Nolan, curate at St. Francis Xaviers', Brooklyn. (Father Nolan is a nephew of Monsignor McGolrick).

When the preacher of the day came down from the pulpit, the celebrant stepped to the altar railing to address a few words of greeting to his people and to the visiting clergy, many of whom had been his Assistants in former years and could remember with him other titular Feastdays. To them he paid tribute. He then briefly recalled the memories of his Seminary days when with the student body of the American College, he marched to and fro St. Cecilia's Church in the Trastevere quarter of Rome to participate in the solemn commemoration of the Saint's martyrdom. Wholly unmindful was he then that almost the entire number of years of his long, long priesthood would be lived under St. Cecilia's special patronage.

During the Offertory of the Mass, Fr. McLoughlin with power and mellow sweetness rendered the solo.

A beautiful Hymn to the patron saint was sung by the Girls' Choir as a Recessional.

PANEGYRIC OF THE PATRON SAINT.

Believing that Father McLoughlin's words will be fruit-ful of good, not only in the hearts of those who listened to them on St. Cecilia's Day, but also in the hearts of those who may read them, the sermon is here transcribed.

"These are they who are come out of great tribulation, and have washed their robes, and have made them white in the blood of the Lamb." (Apocalypse VII. 14).

Today we are assembled to honor one who is high in the long list of martyrs for the faith, who is venerated in the lit-urgy of the universal church, who is the patroness of music, sacred and profane, and who is in a particular way dear to us for she is the heavenly patroness of this our great parish. Under the guidance of your revered pastor and because St. Cecilia besought and obtained God's blessing on his efforts, it has grown to be one of the largest in the diocese of Brook-lyn and can boast of buildings, dedicated to the service of God, which are beautiful and massive and in their silence speak of God's grace poured down in bounteous measure on a thriving congregation. Because we are thus dedicated to Cecilia's lov-ing care, it is our privilege to celebrate in a special manner this day which commemorates her glorious martyrdom on earth and her entry into life eternal. It behooves us, therefore, to recall somewhat of her life and of the significance of the sacrifice which she, amongst many others, willingly made for love of Christ and which has raised her to the dignity of a canonized saint of the Church.

St. Cecilia lived in the first half of the third century of the Christian era. She belonged to a noble Roman family and was raised by her parents in the firm practice of paganism. But

in her youth she secretly became a Catholic, and by vow, consecrated her virginity to God, yet, keeping this secret in her
heart, she was espoused to a nobleman, named Valerian. So
moved was Valerian, when he heard of her promise and of
her determination to persist in its observance that he not alone
consented to her remaining a virgin, but was himself converted
from paganism as was also his brother, Tiburtius. Because of
their firm adherence to the doctrines of Christianity and their
fearless practice of their religious duties, all three were put to
death by the pagan prefect of the city of Rome, one Almachius.
We are told that the executioner let his sword fall three times
without separating Cecilia's head from her body and then fled,
leaving the virgin bathed in her own blood. In this awful
condition, she lived three days and when at last she died, her
body was first buried in the Catacombs of Pope Callistus. Her
relics were later removed to a church, within the city, which
was dedicated to her memory. Since then, many churches in
various parts of the world have been placed under her protection and we surely should be proud today of the beautiful
marble edifice which, under her patronage, is fitting home for
Jesus Christ in our midst.

Even this very brief resume of the life of St. Cecilia,
coupled with what we know of the glorious age of the martyrs, particularly in the City of Rome where our saint met her
end, ought to fill our hearts with thoughts which no tongue
can speak. And what city of the world has for the true Cath-
lic more magic in its name than the city of Rome—the home
of the Vicar of Christ, the fountain-source of our faith, the
last resting-place of so many of the fearless martyrs, who
shed their blood within its walls rather than betray the trust
which God had awakened in their souls: Well might Byron
sing and well might we, with deeper significance, re-echo his
words:

"O Rome, my country, city of the soul,

The orphans of the heart must turn to thee."

The Church of God was not to be confined to one city or
people. It was to embrace all nations and tribes and tongues.
Yet it was to be one spiritual kingdom on earth and its unity
was to be the very proof of the divinity which begot and sus-
tains it. In the ways of providence, Rome, chosen as the centre
of that unity, was to reverse Rome's destiny. Before the advent
of Christianity, Rome was mistress of humanity on land and
sea, the throne of Satan and the centre of a degraded paganism. But with the establishment of Christianity within her
walls, her destiny was changed and she became the spiritual
mother of the faithful sons of Christ in many a clime. During
the first three centuries of Christianity the foundations of this
spiritual city were cemented by the blood of many martyrs.
Every age and condition of life, from gentle maidens of the
type of St. Cecilia to hardy soldiers like St. Sebastian, sent
its chosen champions to the triumph of martyrdom in Rome.
There is no part of the city which is not hallowed by association with this sad but glorious era. The Circus of Nero was
the first great theatre of these triumphs and it was meet that
on this sacred spot the noble shrine of St. Peter's, with its vast
and mighty dome, should raise its pinnacles to the skies. Then
the Colosseum was so steeped in Christian blood that a little
of its dust was carried away by visitors and cherished as a
priceless relic. And around the city, dug deep into the ground,
were built the Catacombs, those mighty bulwarks of the faith,
where the people worshipped unmolested and beneath whose
altars repose the remains of so many of the martyrs. The
martyrdom of St. Cecilia is but one of the glorious events
which grace the history of early Christian Rome and that
heart would indeed be stony which could not be moved by the

heroism which thus inspired a woman to suffer so cruel a death for love of Jesus.

We are all readily impressed by whatever is grand and noble and unselfish. Nobility of soul commands our respect wherever it is found, whether in Church or State. We admire heroism and are impressed by it, no matter what the circumstances in which it is displayed. The world has its heroes just as the Church has hers. We love to see, hear or read of those who have deserved well of their fatherland. The United States is proud of Washington and Lincoln; Rome of Caesar and Pompey; Greece of Leonides and Pericles; Germany of Frederick, the Great, and Bismarck; Ireland of Brian Boru and Sarsfield. And such patriotic and national pride is a good thing and to be commended. But what now of these great names of history and thousands of others of lesser fame? Their bodies have long since mingled with the dust and their souls—we are not certain of their fate nor do we pause for one moment to consider. Their great achievements and worldly success are no passports to eternal glory. We do not wish to detract from their mighty deeds, which may or may not have been inspired by worthy motives. But what do the conquering heroes of the world gain by all their glorious victories? What are these victories in themselves and in their relation to eternity? Shall they avail aught in the final judgment and shall rewards be meted out in proportion to the honor and respect one has achieved in the eyes of his fellowmen? No, dear Brethren; in the eyes of God, these are the true heroes who have conquered not kingdoms but themselves, who with unobtrusive piety have striven to emulate the sublime example of the crucified Saviour. The martyrs, virgins and confessors are in reality the noblest heroes in all history for without the lure of obtaining human glory and without the expectation of the homage of human applause, they sacrificed everything rather than be unfaithful to the call of their Divine Master. Now their names are emblazoned on the Book of Life and they have attained to the reward which Our Lord promised to those who fight the good fight and win the race. Now they are basking, not in the doubtful rays of human favour, but in the sunshine of God's glory and in the unfading light of His divine countenance.

What relation ought there be between us and the Saints of God? Are we merely to admire them from afar and perhaps raise our hearts to them at times in a condescending kind of prayer, which lacks any very deep sense of conviction regarding the power and willingness of the Saints to help us by their intercession? Have the Saints any place in the divine providence planning our salvation and providing us with the means of accomplishing it? Yes, dear Brethren, the saints have been raised up by God, not merely for His own honor and glory, but also to be our models and examples. As such, they alone are worthy of our imitation. But, alas, how few amongst us make any serious or sustained effort to resemble them? No one can deny that a great chasm separates us from them. Yet, both we and they were created for precisely the same eternal destiny; we, too, are called to be saints. What therefore is the reason for the vast difference between us and them?

Doubtless you will suggest that the environment in which we live makes it impossible for us to persist in the practice of virtue. You forget that Cecilia and numerous other saints lived amidst all the corruption of paganism. They, too, were human and, like us, susceptible to all the influences of their surroundings. Environment may be a hindrance but it certainly is not an insurmountable obstacle to the pursuit of sanctity. Nor can the peculiar nature of our calling in life be responsible for holiness is independent of station in life: kings and queens, soldiers and statesmen, leaders and slaves, rich and poor, religious and laity, all have furnished proof that God's grace is effective in all conditions of human life.

No, dear Brethren, the secret of sanctity is something far more personal than mere distinction of environment or calling. The difference between one who is and one who is not a Saint is to be sought, not in the things done, but in the manner in which they are done. The Saints did very much what we do but they went about it in a very different spirit. In the words of St. Paul, whether they ate or drank or whatever else they did, they did all in the name of the Lord Jesus Christ. Their faith was a lively one which influenced their every work and sanctified what they did, because it inspired them with the proper motive. They were guided by the maxims of the Gospel, by the precepts of the Church and by the divine example of the Redeemer. They realized that the grace of God, received through the divine channels of God's sacraments, called for a ready cooperation on the part of the recipient. This then seems to be the fundamental difference between the saints and the ordinary Christian: the one lives rooted to the earth and is so engrossed in the business of life that he has no time to ponder on the meaning of the great eternal truths, of death, of judgment and of eternity which are withal indelibly imprinted on his heart; the other realizes in an intimate way the sublime significance of these truths and because he understands them, he is moved to so order his life that nothing which he does will interfere with his living in God's friendship and thus continually striving for the consummation of life which is to die in grace and be happy with God for ever. If we are to appreciate at all the meaning of such sacrifices as Cecilia made for love of Christ, we, too, as she did, must pause to think of the purpose of our lives here on earth. Having thought and understood, we must realize that practical Catholicity calls for a self-denial which ought to enter into our daily lives and by purging us of affection for the fleeting things of life make us keep ever before our minds as an incentive and an ideal, the life of glory in which, by the goodness of God, we are all called to participate. "Remember thy last end," says the Holy Spirit, "and thou shalt never sin," and it is precisely because we are too material, too selfish and too busy with the affairs of the world to think on our eternal destiny that we lead a blind existence and waste away our weary lives in the pursuit of the phantom treasures of a world that is today, and tomorrow is no more. "With desolation," says the Holy Spirit, "is the whole land made desolate, because there is no one who thinketh in the heart."

The Arabs have a fable that the great pyramid of Egypt, that tremendous monument to a great pagan civilization, was built by their kings before the deluge and that it alone of all the works of men, bore the weight of the flood. Such as this was the fate of the Church in the great age of the martyrs. It had been buried under the great flood of tyranny and hate; but its foundations remained unshaken and when the waters abated it appeared alone amid the ruins of a world which had passed away. The glorious passing of her martyrs has but added new life and vigor to this edifice of Christ, built upon the solid rock of faith. Cecilia too has passed away but her glory and heroism are for ever written on the parchments of eternity and her memory is ever fresh in the history and liturgy of the Church. Today, in many edifices, in many lands, are her spiritual brethren gathered in her honor. We, too, are amongst the number. In this marble church, dedicated to her memory and placed under her protection, are we assembled to honor our patroness and our queen. May she ever watch over us. May she beg God's blessing on your revered pastor who has raised this splendid memorial to her name and to whom under God is committed the care of your souls. May she intercede for those priests who are his helpers in this work of Christ. May she look with kindly eyes on you, whose heavenly guardian she is and move your hearts to a vivd realization of your spiritual destiny. May her example and her prayers ever guide us along the straight and narrow paths of virtue and lead us to the throne of God. May we all one day merit the inestimable privilege of standing with her before the throne of the Good God, there to sing the praises of the Lord with that vast army of white-robed Saints who, crowned with the garland of sanctity, worship at the feet of the Most High. Amen.

ST. CECILIA *by* CARL MADERNO

Beneath the High Altar in St. Cecilia's Church, Rome

REV. EUGENE McLOUGHLIN

REV. HENRY DOHENY   REV. JOHN KRIEG

Assistant Pastors.

The names of the Assistant Pastors who have labored at St. Cecilia's during the Pastorate of Monsignor McGolrick are:

*Rev. Michael J. Malone
*Rev. Michael Flaherty
*Rev. Thomas Duhigg
*Rev. Patrick J. Fahey
*Rev. James McMahon
*Rev. Philip J. Kenny
*Rev. John Kelly
*Rev. H. E. Brady
*Rev. William F. Sheehy
*Rev. John A. Fitzpatrick
 Rev. Timothy Kelleher
 Rev. Dennis R. Carroll
 Rt. Rev. Msgr. Charles F. Gibney
*Rev. William J. Donovan
 Rev. James F. Irwin
 Rev. Jose Rivera
 Rev. Martin J. Biggane
 Rev. M. C. Dempsey
*Rev. Marco Simmonetti

*Rev. Wm. E. Enright, D. D.
*Rev. George Gardiner
 Rev. John T. Burke
 Rev. Leopold A. Arcese
*Rev. Vincent P. Delaney
 Rev. Charles A. Rohr
 Rev. Peter Jessup
 Rev. Thomas Sheehy
 Rev. P. J. Bugler
 Rev. James H. Dolan
 Rev. Patrick J. Manton
 Rev. William H. Jurney
*Rev. Joseph A. McElroy
 Rev. Thos. P. Casey
 Rev. John A. Shea
 Rev. Arthur O'Connor
 Rev. Edmund J. Carey
 Rev. Francis A. Fitzgerald

*Indicates that these priests have gone to their reward.

The present Assistant Pastors are: Rev. Henry Doheny, Rev. John Krieg, Rev. Eugene McLoughlin.

HIGH ALTAR

St. Cecilia Church, Brooklyn, N. Y.

THE INTERIOR BEAUTY OF THE EDIFICE.

A few years ago, the writer was privileged to attend the Mass of Pope Pius XI in the Sistine Chapel on Easter Sunday. Not until the Holy Father and his court had passed down the aisle and out of the Chapel, did I realize in what place I was. The inner eye had been feasting on the "realities of the unseen" and so it was that even Michel Angelo's frescoes, of primary importance on a previous visit to the Sistine, were utterly forgotten in this hour of all too seldom devotion.

A little similar, the experience in St. Cecilia's on this Feast-day. The beautiful music, the colorful ceremonies of the Solemn High Mass, the soul stirring sermon, the vivid picturing of Rome and its familiar holy places, induced that ardour of spirit which is all absorbing. Not until the Mass was over, when only the incense clinging to altar and arch told of the hour that had been, did I fasten attention on the decorative beauties of the interior of the edifice. The windows, the statues, the paintings, the sanctuary lamps, the pulpit, the altar railing, and the stations were one and all in keeping with the dignity and beauty of the architecture.

The statue of St. Joseph is particularly arresting, the voluminous folds of the robe create an artistic, graceful effect not often seen in other presentations of the subject. This statue and that of the Blessed Virgin and the Sacred Heart are of Caen stone and are the work of Joseph Sibbel.

The tablet to which the Manhattan classmate refers reads: "This way of the Cross is erected to the glory of God and for a lasting memorial of Peter McGolrick, a benefactor of this Church."

Many of the paintings are copies of twelfth century Irish mural decorations.

SHRINE OF OUR LADY OF PERPETUAL HELP

The Shrine of Our Lady of Perpetual Help.

In the struggling years when there rested a heavy debt upon the Church, a painting of Our Lady of Perpetual Help was brought to St. Cecilia's by a Sister of Mercy. It was hung in the Sacristy and in public and private devotions, the intercession of Our Lady was sought.

Later, when the happy day of consecration of the building was realized, the painting was used as centrepiece of a shrine erected in honor of Our Lady's powerful aid.

The picture is set in a rectangular mosaic frame and this, in turn, is framed by a great central arch of mosaic work. On either side are lesser arched panels and in further there are simulated pillars paneled in mosaic decoration.

In the great central arch, blue and gold prevail, and the tesserae are of luminous beauty set in elaborate design. The arch proper is centered with a cross.

The votive candles, always burning before the shrine, testify to the people's great devotion to the Virgin Mary under this her most hope-giving title—Our Lady of Perpetual Help.

THE BAPTISTRY

St. Cecilia's Church

The Baptistry.

The Baptistry is of exceptional beauty. Public entrance leads from Herbert Street. There are also entrances from the front hall of the Rectory and the Church.

Within the terminal arch is placed the central feature of the room, the magnificently carved Baptismal Font. Bas-relief figures decorate the lower part of the Font, the central group showing St. John baptizing Our Lord. The marble paneling around the wall of the room is elevated in the arched recess and to give further unity of composition, the central portion of this paneling is capped with an arch. This brings the surmounting cross of the Font into commanding relievo.

The recess wall above the marble wainscoting is frescoed with picture of our Lord's baptism, adoring angels hovering near. A cross, patterned of varying dark marbles, forms full length central decoration in the tesselated floor, while circling the base of the Font is symbolic crown design.

Stained windows bestow cathedral light. The benches are of carved walnut. Their number tells a heartening story. Whatever the world may be preaching and teaching to the contrary, it is quite evident St. Cecilia's mothers are obeying God's law in regard to the welcoming of offspring. And it is indeed fitting that their babies' Baptistry should be a place of beauty. It is within this room the babies' souls are cleansed from original sin, making them children of God and heirs of heaven.

RT. REV. MONSIGNOR EDWARD J. McGOLRICK

Rector, St. Cecilia's Church

RIGHT REV. MONSIGNOR EDWARD J. McGOLRICK.

From that rainy day when Father McGolrick for the first time "plodded up Herbert Street" on his way to the only passtoral charge he has thus far known, one may readily gather knowledge of the man's physical energy and courage and of the priest's spiritual zeal. The magnificent church and numerous other substantial buildings belonging to the parish and erected in his time give testimony of the one and the many educational and charitable activities carrying on under his leadership, as well as the spirit of unity and sterling faith prevailing among his parishioners offer satisfying evidence.

But what of him in the years before that eventful day—the boy, the collegian, the seminarian, the curate? And what of him in relation to society at large and to charitable and educational interests reaching beyond the confines of the parish? His early life proves indeed the truth of the old saying, "the boy is father to the man."

Edward Joseph McGolrick was born May 9, 1857, in that great nursery of scholars and saints, the Isle of Destiny, "found in the track of the setting sun," called by its people Eire and by the Danes, Ireland. The parish of Dunnoughmore, his birthplace, is situated in the historic county of Donegal and in the Diocese of Derry. In the nearest "Chapel" is recorded his baptism, likewise that of his two brothers and three sisters. The McGolrick family were well rooted in the parish of Dunnoughmore for both Peter McGolrick, the father, and Anne Gallagher, the mother, were natives there, of sterling lineage. The village schoolmaster, Peter McGolrick, was godfather for the baby Edward Joseph.

In the local school of his native parish, the boy first drank from learning's crystal stream and when, in 1865, the entire family moved to America to occupy the comfortable home in Brooklyn which the provident father had already built and furnished for them, he became a pupil in St. James' parochial school in Jay Street. Upon the completion of the grammar course, he entered Manhattan College, New York, and graduated from that excellent institution 'cum laude' in the class of 1877.

At the commencement exercises of the Class of '77, the first American Cardinal presided for the first time and it was a signal mark of honor that fell to our young graduate to deliver the address of welcome. To the multitudes who through the long intervening years have heard the zealous preacher, and to other tens of thousands who have sat beneath the spell of Monsignor McGolrick's forceful, erudite, witty, platform eloquence, this his maiden attempt at public oratory, may coax a smile but for the young man of that day it was an occasion of great import, of deadly seriousness, parents, teachers, friends and class-mates hanging breathless on his words and the Cardinal listening.

Address to John Cardinal McCloskey.

"You have assembled here this afternoon to witness the graduation exercises of the Class of '77 and to cheer by your presence our initiatory step in life's journey. The great number we see before us gives earnest that there are many eager to extend to us a hearty sympathy in the various undertakings which make this day a landmark in our earthly career. Manhattan's sons who have preceded us have met with a like warm reception and with them as our examples, we have every reasonable assurance that success will crown the efforts of our life. Their course enkindles in us the hope that our aspirations will be realized. They day on which a young man bids farewell to his college home is among the most eventful of his life; it is looked forward to with the greatest anxiety, hailed with gladness, and thought of ever afterwards with feelings of deep emotion. When in after life any of us shall have occasion to pluck a flower from memory's garland what blossom will be more fragrant than that which this after-noon shall contribute. We are heartily thankful for the honor conferred upon us by the presence of so many whose labors are identified with the progress of our holy Religion, whose names are to us household words, venerable men who have grown gray in the service of the Lord. But the greatest honor that we experience today is to behold here one to whom mil-lions of souls look with feeling of love, respect and submis-sion. We not only feel thankful for his presence, but are filled with sentiments of just pride and gratitude for it is not emi-nently fitting that our hearts should overflow with thankfulness on beholding among us a citizen of our beloved land, whose virtues have earned for him the highest dignity in the gift of Mother Church. No courtly influence, no princely solicitations worked his elevation for thank God, nothing but loftiness of character, the possession of shining virtue, profound learning and undying zeal for the salvation of souls are in our day the exclusive passports to Ecclesiastical dignity and preferment. This honor is doubly enhanced, crowned it is with brightest lustre when viewed as coming from the hands of one of the grandest and holiest pontiffs that ever sat on the chair of Peter. Gratitude would hold an inferior place in our breasts were we to remain insensible of the great honor conferred upon us by the presence of a prince of the Church. The spirit that prompts our welcome to him is not that which moves the world to hold the presence of worldly magnates, the titled and wealthy ones of the earth. Our welcome partakes not of the spirit of the world as children of the Church we are unspeakably grate-ful for the countless favors she has bestowed upon us, we wel-

come him from the bottom of our hearts as a son of that venerable mother whom she has been pleased to distinguish as the
highest representative of the Church on the shores of the Western hemisphere. What child upon his first feeble attempt at
the prosecution of life's labor does not delight in the smile of
a loving father, the encouraging look, the approving word, the
glance of pleasure which lights that Father's eyes are ever
held in view as treasures of inestimable value. And doubly
dear is the kindness exhibited by him in being present in our
midst as he thus encourages our first feeble flutterings along
life's checkered pathway and furnishes us with a fresh incentive to persevere in our noble undertakings. His office does
not indeed entail upon him the duty of attending college com-
mencements, still the great desire that burns in his soul for
the promotion of Christian education—"Education that is
sublime in its motive, exalted in its means and divine in its
ends"—makes this though an irksome still a pleasing task,
since such an education is the primary and at the same time
the most important means toward the advancement of the
cause to which he has devoted his life. In after life, when deep
in the cares of the world, it will be the greatest honor for us
members of the Class of '77 to be able to say that we received
our diplomas from his hands. Yes, when the bright dreams
of college life shall have been dispelled by the chilling blasts
of actual experience; when, perchance, our grand projects
shall have failed, then will the thought of this day spring up
with new life to cheer and encourage to renewed endeavors,
as the welcome light of the harbor beacon cheers and guides
the tempest tossed mariner to a port of safety.

Venerable Cardinal, it is my very pleasing duty, speaking
on behalf of the students and professors of Manhattan College
and their friends here assembled, to bid you thrice welcome."

What a Manhattan Classmate Writes.

Only three of the boys of that class of '77 are now living. I have asked one of them to write for this book his impressions of his classmate's character in boyhood years. In enthusiastic manner, he has written more, but I am not willing to blue pencil his reply. He writes:

"How well I remember Eddie McGolrick in dear old Manhattan. In the classroom he showed the practical as well as the ideal. Even then he seemed to sense that the world deals more largely in the one than in the other. His compositions were always in prose but a prose that hinted at the fine poetry of his thought. Here we have an augery of the future builder, such a builder as has changed the wilderness of forty years ago into a garden spot, wherein flower hospital, lyceum, convent, monastery, school, library, day nursery and marble basilica. Eddie was born, as you know, in that section of Ireland where the Four Masters toiled through patient years to bring to life the buried treasures of Irish history.

> These shattered walls once sheltered light
> That lit the way to treasures rare.
> A nation's story, screened from sight,
> The Masters Four, all learned, bare.
> Pompeian splendors pale in troth
> Before the marvels they disclose,
> All dug from ashes despots wrought.
> Inspired anew, old Eire rose,
> With racial pride she walked a Queen,
> Bedecked with history's jewelled page,
> Then, Phoenix-like, she soared between
> Her martyred dead, her living sage.
> The land all wondering blessed the power
> That from oblivion brought her name,

> And widowed Eire won her dower
> When History added Eire's fame.

Eddie was a great reader. Inspired to this by the principle in the Azarius philosophy he studied, 'Thought begets thought.' As a young Irishman he easily leaned toward the classics and religion. This two-fold inclination went steadily on to his seminary course in the great classic and religious centre of the world—*Rome*. It is living still in virile force in the priest and scholar whose religious and classic volumes are thumbed in constant use and constructive thought.

He had an enthusiastic love for outdoor sports and was quite a figure in Manhattan's baseball nine. I can see him when after wholesome play he returned breathless to the classroom with the red of health in his cheeks and the enthusiasm of honest, happy boyhood in his heart. I, who saw him thus in life's morning hours, have never wondered at his continuing interest in athletics. The McGolrick Recreation Field in St. Cecilia's Parish is but a practical evidence of his entrenched belief—"A sound mind in a sound body."

In Manhattan, he was always happy-hearted. He never profaned his face with a sneer. Always witty, he enjoyed a joke and laughed loudest when entertained with one. His laugh was infectious, so that it struck the keynote for many. In this, he showed the naturally buoyant, mirthful quality of the Irish heart.

But for all his love of fun, his spirit was ever deeply reverential towards his teachers. And what teachers he had! The literary brillance of Azarius illumined his text; the profundity of Potamium's scientific learning dwelt in the classroom, satisfying the student that the lights of religion are the lamps of science; the majestic character of Anthony turned boyhood feet toward heights of sterling honor; the eloquence of

Humphrey, whose power Edwin Booth recognized, taught his tongue the wizard's way; the quiet, gentle force of President Pauline, whose example indelibly impressed his high character as a gentleman upon us all, was ever before him as a model.

Not only did his mind gain College training at Manhattan, but his heart was there developed by the high and holy principles of religion. The Christian Brothers are grand exponents of the sublimity of simplicity. Humble and unassuming, they are doing most when apparently doing least. Power radiates from their seclusion. We never met men who carried so much of the heart of childhood into manhood. We never conversed with men so foreign to their own greatness. We never met kings of human-kind such absolute strangers to dress parade. Unseeking, they are ever sought; blind to their own deserts, they have a quick eye for others' worth; humble, they scorn its ugly mockery—Uriah Heap 'umbleness.' With unbounded faith, they walk down life's valley conscious that they are never alone if with Christ. These the teachers, and these the high qualities impressed upon and admired by the plastic heart of the boy, so that admiration naturally turned to emulation which grew with his growth and flowered with his experience.

Needless to say, the boy who was to be the future honored and worthy priest had no black marks against his character or conduct and if, occasionally, he did penance "at the clock" it was for nothing worse than an outburst of mirth in the study hall, a misdemeanor never countenanced by the sedate Brother Jasper.

When packing for vacation, his greatest joy was anticipation of delightful home associations. He had a brave adventurous father and a quiet prayerful mother. The boy himself reflected the courageous daring of the one and the religious gentleness of the other.

ANNE GALLAGHER McGOLRICK

Mother of Monsignor McGolrick

PETER McGOLRICK
Father of Monsignor McGolrick

What a man was his father! And how eventful his life!
Add to his Donegal sturdiness of character which lost not itself in idle complaining, he had great fortitude and pushed
steadily onward and upward toward success. His persistent
efforts overcame apparently insurmountable obstacles.   On
landing in New York, he lost no time in pursuing his journey
to the Gold Mines of California. Across the Isthmus he tramped
his way. When his shoes wore out, he trod on barefoot, although as he himself said quaintly, "There were plenty of
dead men's shoes but I wouldn't wear them."

This brand of heroism in the father shows again in the son
who has carved out his own way not following precedent's
failures. The father's generosity was ever an encouragement
to the young priest building St. Cecilia's, but however great
Peter McGolrick's material benefactions to the parish, they
pale in comparison to the spirit he passed on to its pastor—
the spirit of fortitude and perseverance. Small wonder then
that as a priest Monsignor McGolrick is a model, bold and
tireless in effort, gracious in manner, refined in expression,
powerful in pulpit, and ever and always conscious is he that
the Altar is another Calvary. He has learned how to make
sacrifices and so he is a priest in heart and deed. Nothing
of the good and great that is found today in the Domestic
Prelate, Monsignor McGolrick, surprises me who was with
him at Manhattan and can remember his parents and the bright
promise his boyhood gave."

After Manhattan.

In the summer of 1877, the Manhattan graduate sailed
away from New York Harbor. He was on his way to Rome.
His father accompanied him as far as Ireland, where, together
they enjoyed a revival of early memories, and where, the
young Seminarian in the making called upon the Bishop of
Derry, the Bishop of his native diocese.

He entered the American College in Rome in October, 1877. In the Souvenir booklet commemorating the Silver Jubilee of the Pastor of St. Cecilia's, we read the words of a cherished companion of his Seminary days, one who now ranks high indeed in the educational and Church life of America, the Right Rev. Bishop Shahan of Washington, D. C., President Emeritus of the Catholic University.

"During your pastor's years of study at the American College, he was distinguished for his constant good humor and kindly bearing toward all. It is remembered to this day by his companions that not an unpleasant word escaped him and that he never exhibited any of those breaks of temper that are so common among the young and inexperienced. His devotion to study was irreproachable, and he always stood well in the examinations and competitions that marked the close of the year's study in the Propaganda College. He was particularly beloved by the students of the other English speaking colleges (the Irish, English and Scotch) who never failed to seek him out when they met the American students in any one of the Roman villas that were then, as now, the haunts of the young ecclesiastics during their hours of recreation. He was even then a man of solid principle and perfect honor, in whom all his juniors were wont to confide, and whom all his superiors considered in every way trustworthy and exemplary."

For five years he pursued his studies for the priesthood in the American College and was ordained in the Cathedral of Rome, the Church of St. John Lateran, by his Eminence Cardinal Monaco La Veletta, June 3rd, 1882. Fr. McGolrick's father and a brother-in-law, Mr. Lawrence McGolrick journeyed to the Eternal City to be present at the ordination.

On the return of the young Levite to America and to the diocese for which he had been ordained, he was assigned by the Right Rev. Bishop Loughlin to St. Patrick's Church as curate. The Pastor of St. Patrick's at the time was the Rev. Thomas Taaffe, native of Ireland, and educated at All Hallows College, who had come to Brooklyn in 1864. Father Taaffe's pastorate at St. Patrick's extended over a period of thirty-five years. He was a priest of outstanding mental and spiritual attainments and an untiring and uncomplaining worker in Christ's vineyard.

When a boy, Father McGolrick, as acolyte in St. James' Cathedral, frequently served Bishop Loughlin's Mass and now, at the beginning of his sacredotal ministry, he was to be the recipient of a signal service from the Bishop, namely, an appointment as curate to St. Patrick's, for at St. Patrick's he was to gain an indelible close-up of those qualities of mind and heart that make for a worthy shepherd of souls. Monsignor McGolrick looks back in a spirit of lively gratitude upon the time he was privileged to spend under the guidance of Father Taaffe. This, his first and only curacy, lasted six years. Then came his appointment as Pastor of St. Cecilia's. In the life of any Curate, his promotion to a Pastoral charge is a thrilling experience. So it was for Father McGolrick when, on that November day in 1888, full of hope and joy and pride and indomitable courage, he made his way to St. Cecilia's. The heavy rain might dampen his clothes but neither it, nor the dilapidated buildings he found waiting his arrival, could dampen the spirit of Peter McGolrick's son. He was a Pastor now and a Pastor's work he meant to do. Into the little Church he went; the roof was leaking badly; he brushed aside intruding discouragement and knelt to ask humanity's Unfailing Friend to guide and help him in the work there was to do, knowing that without Christ's hand and helping grace naught of worth could be accomplished. From that first hour unto the present he has thrown his whole heart and strength into collossal undertakings for the honor and glory of God and the salvation of souls,—thrown heart and strength and a smile. The smile, that made lasting impression on Manhattan and Roman classmate alike, continues to be a tangible asset to the pastor of St. Cecelia's in the great work of directing a parish and in his dealings with the world at large. Besides this, it has kept his own nature boyish and unsoured through the years, and ever ready for more work. To those who grumble when the way seems hard he invariably counsels, "Work, for work like fasting is God's medicine. It makes us forget and it helps to steady our nerves."

That his cheerful bearing rests on religion is disclosed in a letter to one who complained of the pain of ingratitude 'sharper than a serpent's tooth.' "As we go on in years," wrote the Monsignor, "ingratitude makes a great wound in our hearts. Let us accept such and bear it through love of Him who complained of nothing that He suffered."

Mother Church and Alma Mater have bestowed on the Pastor of St. Cecilia's honors well-deserved; the one making him Domestic Prelate, the other Doctor of Laws and Trustee of Manhattan College. In today's Monsignor is found the same reverence for the Christian Brothers as lived in the collegiate's heart. A few years ago, he acted as Chairman of the "New Manhattan Drive" and needless to say, exampled by his generosity and zeal, the Drive was a success.

At the last meeting of the Board of Trustees of the Catholic University of America, November 18, 1930, Monsignor McGolrick was elected a member of that body. To have voice in the deliberations of America's most distinguished educational Board is a supreme tribute to the character and learning of the Pastor of St. Cecilia's—a tribute, in which his devoted and united people feel a just pride. With all the stress and strain of caring for a great parish, of making that parish a really outstanding one in our country, the boy nature in the man has found time for recreative travel and has always returned the Pastor to the serious labors of his life promptly, cheerily and with renewed energy.

Nor does he believe that any man has the right to sink into the lap of years fully content with what has been accomplished for always there is work still to be done. He believes that work is the panacea for half life's ills and an excellent preparation for eternity's joy. His spirit of effort and optimism is best expressed in the words written by himself in a recent letter to a friend of boyhood days—he begins with the salutation: "Dear old friend" and then promptly adds: "When I had written that salutation I said to myself, that is wrong. We are not old. We are still young in heart as we were fifty years ago, still hopeful, still planning great things for the future."

And that is the keynote to the character of the present Monsignor McGolrick. He is still youthful in heart, still hopeful of what may be achieved for good among his people, still planning great things for St. Cecilia's, and still remembering that without God's help and guidance nothing of good can come to him or to his flock. With Newman he prays:

May He support us all the day long, till the shades lengthen, and the evening comes, and the busy world is hushed, and the fever of life is over, and our work is done! Then in His mercy may He give us a safe lodging, and a holy rest, and peace at the last!

—*Cardinal Newman.*

ABOUT THE AUTHOR*

AGNES B (CHUTE) KING, author and lecturer, was born in Titus-ville, PA in 1879. She was one of seven children born to Robert Chute (County Cork, Ireland) and Elizabeth Higgins (PA). After her birth the family moved to Cleveland, Ohio where Agnes was educated and later became a teacher. In 1913, she married William A. King; they had three children: Sheila, William, and Edward. Following her husband's death, she moved to Ironton, Ohio, where for 6 years she wrote a column for the *Catholic Columbian* (Columbus, OH). In 1920 Agnes went to Ireland to visit her father's ancestral home in County Cork. On her return to the US, she was invited to testify before the Howe Commission in Washington, DC. about the conditions and treatment of the Irish in County Cork, Ireland (*The Nation*, Vol III, No 2893, page 715–16). In Washington she met Fr. McGolrick, who later invited her to visit his parish in Brooklyn, NY. During her visit to St. Cecilia's Parish, she decided to chronicle the story of Father McGolrick, then Msgr. McGolrick, in *The Story of a Rare Parish* (1931). Prior to the completion of this book, Agnes published *Real Christian Science*, *Brief Life of Sister Augustine, IHM*, and a novel, *Duncan Davidson* (1928). She was also a well–known lecturer who spoke throughout the US and Canada, and in Galway, Rome, and Havana. She passed away in 1957 in Ironton, Ohio.

---

* Primary Source: *American Catholic Who's Who* (CWW7, pg. 231). Agnes is also listed in: *Ohio Authors and Their Books: Biographical Data and Selective Bibliographies for Ohio Authors, Native and Resident, 1796–1950*

www.ingramcontent.com/pod-product-compliance
Lightning Source LLC
Chambersburg PA
CBHW031836090426
42741CB00005B/267